SOUTH DERBYSHIRE AND ITS PEOPLE:
A HISTORY

Wash day in Castle Gresley. 1913

Courtesy of Beryl Greening

SOUTH DERBYSHIRE
AND ITS PEOPLE:
A HISTORY

by
Oswald Hull

Derbyshire County Council
Cultural & Community Services Department
2004

Published by
Derbyshire County Council Cultural & Community Services Department.

© 2004 Oswald Hull

A note on the illustrations:
Except where stated otherwise the illustrations in the book are taken from
Derbyshire Library collections. Many of them are available to view and
purchase on Picture the Past: a website of Derbyshire and Nottinghamshire
photographs. www.picturethepast.org.uk

ISBN: 0 903463 75 X

Front cover:
TL Murray's Map 1831
Market Hall and Delph, Swadlincote
Courtesy HJ Wain

Back cover:
Sir Peter de Gresley, died about 1310

Design & Production:
Country Books, Courtyard Cottage, Little Longstone, Derbyshire DE45 1NN

Printed & Bound in England by:
Antony Rowe Ltd

CONTENTS

ACKNOWLEDGEMENTS

In compiling this history, I have received help from a number of local sources, notably Dr. Margaret O'Sullivan, County and Diocesan Archivist for Derbyshire and Dr. Martin Sanders, Archivist in Charge for Staffordshire. I have used items from the Local Studies Library in Derby, the Swadlincote and Burton-on-Trent Libraries and the William Salt Library in Stafford. Janet Spavold, editor of an important history of Church Gresley, has read and made many helpful comments on my text and Colin Kitching of Repton, Dr. Joan D'Arcy of Derby and Jeff Clinton of Shardlow have provided me with other valuable assistance.

I have drawn heavily on the National Archives at Kew, particularly as regards 19th century workhouses and have also consulted the national Family Records Centre in London and both the book and manuscript collections of the British Library.

I am greatly obliged to Jeremy Hull who drew the maps and graphs, to Jane Connor for organising the most complicated of the diagrams and Christopher Hull for his skill in pulling the final threads together. Caroline Walton produced the first computerised text and Alena Jefferies the final version.

I have had encouragement and help from Philip Heath, Heritage Officer for South Derbyshire and Graham Nutt of Swadlincote's Magic Attic Archive whilst, I have throughout been able to rely on the essential support and strength of Mrs. Ruth Gordon, Local Studies Librarian at County Hall, Matlock.

INTRODUCTION

The South Derbyshire covered by this book is the district administered since 1974 from Swadlincote. Before it was divided into counties, the region had been part of Mercia. Derby was a former Roman settlement and Derbyshire's borders survived the Norman Conquest. In the Domesday Survey, Swadlincote and Melbourne were named, but not Gresley. The most important Norman knights in South Derbyshire were of de Stafford or de Ferrers stock.

Christianity came south from Northumbria but Repton, the Mercian capital, was unsafe with Vikings in possession of Derby, and its bishop's seat was moved to Lichfield. At times of famine and distress, a peasant would seek alms from the nearest religious house, a line of relief that would eventually be severed by the ambition of a king.

Under Henry VIII, the priories of Gresley and Repton were investigated by agents acting on behalf of the all-powerful ruler, who then seized the wealth of the religious houses and destroyed many of their buildings. After the Reformation, there followed a period of unparalleled religious strife when anyone advocating the wrong religion could be put to death. 'Papist hunters' were active under Elizabeth I and my story includes a notable encounter in the next reign with a household of Catholics in Castle Gresley. Nonconformists, including Methodists, were permitted to meet in designated houses and eventually become more and more influential throughout the district.

Tudor monarchs in principle accepted responsibility for anyone who starved, but it was ordered that vagrants could be punished merely for idleness and then sent to another parish. The cost of relief grew, nevertheless, and a basic Poor Law of 1601, laying down the rates of relief to be distributed by Overseers of the Poor, lasted until Victorian times.

New tools and alterations to working practice during the 18th century helped to produce changes in a society that had always been farm-based, encouraging enterprise that enriched large operators, and speeding the enclosure of scattered farm holdings. Many land workers' homes were found in the 1860's to be in very poor condition. In South Derbyshire men with capital invested in spectacular new industrial opportunities, and the output of the coalfield was carried away, by tramway, canal and by rail. There was a movement of population from north to south of the area.

New pressures on relief, caused by economic change and a general rise in population, called for an amended Poor Law. Union Boards were set up to control workhouses planned for Burton-on-Trent, Shardlow and Ashby-de-la-Zouch. Conditions in such institutions were deliberately oppressive, to deter the 'undeserving poor'. Some detail is given here about the conditions, illustrated by the statistics for the three local Unions in the year 1851.

Later sections of the book deal with the results of the extension of the franchise by the Reform Bill of 1831 that produced great excitement among all classes. Forster's Education Act of 1871 introduced schooling for all, and then, in the next century, came a new tier of secondary schools. After the war of 1914-18 women were given the vote. By the end of this story, a pottery industry that had started with local clay deposits continued to flourish, but deep mining of coal first declined, and then ceased altogether. Then in a new development at Burnaston, a Japanese car company arrived, continuing the Derby area's long association with vehicle assembly and manufacture.

A NOTE ABOUT

WEIGHTS, MEASURES AND CURRENCY

Throughout the book weights and measures are quoted as they were at the time. So that the reader today can have an idea of the amounts being quoted some comparisons are given.

LAND MEASUREMENTS

Virgates and bovates were very variable quantities of land depending on the quality of the soil.

1 virgate = 2 bovates
1 bovate = 10-20 acres
1 acre = 0·405 of a hectare
NB even acres were not, in early times, a fixed measurement but depended on local custom.
1 yard = 0.914 metres
1 foot = 30.48 centimetres
1 inch = 2.54 centimetres

WEIGHTS

1 hundredweight = 50.8 kilograms
1 pound (lb) = 0.4536 kilograms
1 ounce = 28.35 grams

MONEY

1 guinea = 21 shillings
£1 = 20 shillings or 240 old pence
5 new pence = 1 shilling or 12 old pence
1 new penny = 2.4 old pence

It is very difficult to compare what money was worth then and now but as a rough guide:
In 1264 £1.00 had the purchasing power of £740.73 today

in 1500 = £655.14
in 1600 = £135.16
in 1750 = £105.06
in 1850 = £64.00
in 1950 = £19.25

These figures are taken from:
John J. McCusker, "Comparing the Purchasing Power of Money in Great Britain from 1264 to Any Other Year Including the Present" Economic History Services, 2001, URL : http://www.eh.net/hmit/ppowerbp/

CHAPTER 1

BEFORE THE CONQUEST

GEOLOGY AND SOIL

There is a broad band of alluvium along the valleys of the Trent, Dove and lower Derwent, with the rest of South Derbyshire underlain by Coal Measures (east of Newhall), Keuper Sands and Bunter Beds (surrounding the coal area) and Keuper Marl in the Mease-Seal country on the Leicestershire border.

The Bunter Pebble Beds demand a lot of work from the farmer, whereas the Keuper Marl west of Linton is a good red soil. Some of the roads in the south follow low ridges of Boulder Clay and Glacial Sand.

South of the Trent around Melbourne and Stanton by Bridge lies an inlier of Millstone Grit, weathering down to a good dark loam soil, long known throughout the Midlands for its fertility and market garden crops.

GEOLOGY, DRAINAGE AND SETTLEMENT

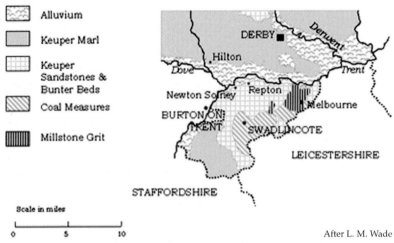

The floodplains that invited settlement continued into Staffordshire

EARLY SETTLEMENT

Romans arrived in the area of the present South Derbyshire on their way to investigate the presence of valuable minerals to the south of the Peak. They decided on the site for a settlement at the mouth of the Derwent valley where there was good access to north and south. About AD 71 a fort – Derventio – was built on the east bank of the Derwent (within the boundary of to-day's Derby), to be followed by a largely civilian settlement on the west bank. A road, Rykneld Street, led from the south towards the Derwent valley opening. It followed the left bank of the Trent without having to cross it, inside the present Derbyshire.

Repton, on a bluff overlooking the Trent floodplain, lies at the end of a narrow valley pointing south in the direction of the South Derbyshire coalfield. From Repton there is good access along the riverside. On the north bank Weston-on-Trent is on a substantial rise and west of Repton is Newton Solney on a low terrace at the very edge of the Trent valley. Early Repton had the advantage of its more raised position overlooking a relatively narrow part of the flood plain and near to a possible crossing point of the river. Further upstream, and more accessible from the north, the river could be forded at Walton by men on horseback. At Winshill a settlement was put down well above river level but before a bridge was built to Burton on the north side.

Soil type could be critical to early settlement:, light soils were more attractive because they were easier to work. Repton and Newton Solney, both backed by higher ground, were built on sand. South of the plain, in the direction of the coalfield, there was a choice between sand and clay sites, where preference was usually given to sand, rather than to the adjacent cap of boulder clay. Further west, Bretby stands on a well-drained site in a large area of sand. Some settlers had either to find a break in the native woodland or themselves make a large enough clearance in which to build their huts.

When the Danes penetrated from the east, and there was

a choice between clay and sand, they chose sand. Smisby, one of the many East Midland settlements with a Danish foundation, lies on sand between Boulder Clay and Coal Measures. South of Gresley the Keuper Marls were improved in areas where they had gravelly drift to provide an excellent medium for the arable farmer.

The kings of Mercia needed, but lacked, easily defensible boundaries. Offa built a spectacular dyke in the West, but rivers of the eastern plains – especially at flood tide – bore Danish invaders in their long boats far inland to colonise the East Midlands.

SAINTS AND ACHIEVERS

In AD 635, Oswald, Christian King of Northumbria, made a decision that was ultimately to be decisive for the development of the Church in Derbyshire, when he invited an Irish priest, Aidan, to join him, to found a bishopric and help to build a monastic school on the island of Lindisfarne.

In AD 653 Paeda, son of the heathen King Penda of Mercia, married Elfleda, King Oswald's daughter, a condition of the marriage being that Christian missionaries be allowed to travel south to Repton. Royal power was crucial in establishing the conditions that would assist the faith. Four priests crossed the Trent here, one of whom was Chad.

A native of Northumberland, Chad had as a boy attended the Lindisfarne school, the curriculum of which included close study of the Gospels in Latin, arithmetic and astronomy.[1] Wulfther, Christian King of Mercia, had requested a new bishop for Mercia and Chad had been chosen. He held office at Repton for only a year before transferring the bishop's seat to the larger and more secure settlement of Lichfield, where he succumbed in AD 672 to the plague that had already killed many other priests. Only in the 14th century was Chad sanctified, with his inclusion in the calendar of English saints that was kept in Canterbury.

It was around AD 660 that the Mercian royal family

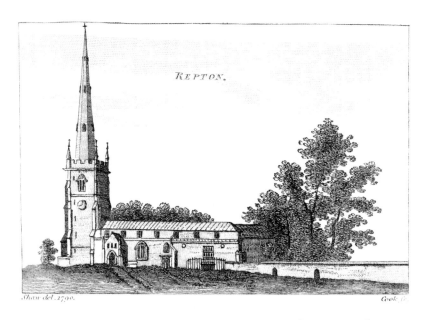

Repton church in 1770. It dates from Saxon times but the visible architecture is principally Norman and later.

established Repton Abbey, a Benedictine religious house for monks and nuns, ruled over by a succession of abbesses that included St. Werbergh and Aelfritha. Archaeological digging between 1974 and 1988 revealed traces of the Abbey and of the adjacent Saxon church. The building of Repton's crypt (or royal mausoleum) by King Ethelbald has been dated to about AD 725. From the Anglo-Saxon Chronicle and other sources it is known that Ethelbald himself was entombed in the crypt in AD 757, as were King Wiglaf in 840 and his grandson, who became St. Wystan, in 850. Concerning the word 'entombed', it is necessary to point out that members of the royal family were not interred in the crypt, but at death were buried elsewhere until the flesh had gone, at which point the skull and major bones were put in caskets of wood or iron. Finally the caskets were placed in the crypt recesses. Originally the crypt

9

was a free-standing chamber, with a low wooden roof, sited slightly east of the church and it was during the reign of King Wiglaf (827-40) that the crypt and the east end of the church were brought together through the building of the chancel. Excavations in the 1970s seemed to confirm that they were there before the Vikings came south via Derby, crossing the Trent in AD 873 to winter in Repton. On leaving, they first burned down Repton's wooden church and the abbey, but the crypt and chancel survived.

To escape the Vikings, the bones of St. Wystan had been taken to a place of safety; later they were brought back to Repton, but were then carried to Evesham during the troubled reign of Danish King Canute (1016-35): St. Wystan's is Repton's parish church today. After the Viking plunder and destruction, the Mercian King Burghred fled to Rome, bringing to an end a dynasty that had eventually found Repton and Britain too dangerous.

The English hold was insecure and in 1013 the Danes conquered all of the country but three years later the English elected the Danish Canute as their king. When Canute died in 1035 the country was ruled by his sons until 1042, when Edward the Confessor was crowned. When he died, there was an invasion by a large Norwegian army, which King Harold defeated at Stamford Bridge.

But greater crisis now threatened, when a Norman army, made up largely of men with Norse origins, assembled under Duke William near the coast of France. Duke William's better prepared force, his archers and crossbow-men giving them the edge over the English, landed in Pevensey Bay on Thursday, 28 September 1066, marched inland to Battle and on 14 October fought and won a struggle afterwards called the Battle of Hastings.

---

1   Austerberry, Jennie, Chad, Bishop and Saint, English Life Publications: Derby, 1984, p. 4.

CHAPTER 2

KINGS AND OTHER RULERS

THE NORMAN SETTLEMENT

Duke William's victory had been complete, with many thousands of King Harold's knights slain along with their leader. What now mattered most to William was the security of his new realm. When, early in his reign, a rebellion or series of rebellions occurred in Mercia, they were put down with the greatest severity. The South Derbyshire districts that were then ravaged by royal decree were five vills: Smisby, Ravenstone, Donisthorpe, Oakthorpe and Thringstone – mostly in a detached part of Derbyshire now within Leicestershire.

In an insecure world William had to be mindful of an over-assertive Pope. He therefore set down markers, instructing that no legislation be proposed by any council of the English church without royal approval. He wished to be, said Stenton, not the Pope's minister but his 'collaborator and ally'.[1] For Archbishop he chose Lanfranc, an eminent cleric from Caen in Normandy who had been born in Pavia. Lanfranc was strong on church government and let his position be known that there had been too many Englishmen sanctified.[2]

Given the presence about him of enemies and doubters William soon set about building a war chest, beginning with an assessment of the land that he had conquered. This culminated in the Domesday Survey of 1086, showing for each owner's parcel of land its acreage, land use and tax payable to the Crown.

A good example of the way the survey was carried out was Aston-on-Trent. It was partly in the royal manor of Weston, a piece in the chain of settlements on the north bank of the Trent that extended from Weston to Shardlow and had

EXTRACT FROM DOMESDAY BOOK
DESCRIBING WESTON AND ASTON ON TRENT

[facsimile of Domesday Book manuscript text]

MANERIUM. In WESTVNE habuit Algar x. carucatas terræ et ii. bouatas et dimidiam ad geldum. Terra totidem carucarum. Ibi nunc in dominio iii. carucæ et xxiiij. uillani et vi. bordarii habentes xii. carucas . et iiij. censarii reddentes xvi. solidos. Ibi ii. æcclesiæ et presbyter et i. molinum xix. solidorum et iiij. denariorum et piscina et passagium aquæ . xiij. solidorum et iiij. denariorum et Li. acræ prati. Pascua dimidia levva longitudine . et iii. Tempore Regis Edwardi viij. libras . modo vi. libras. [quarentenæ latitudine.

Berewitæ hujus Manerii.

BEREWITÆ. In ÆSTUN et SERDELAU vi. bouatæ terræ et dimidia ad geldum. Ibi i. caruca in dominio . et iiij. uillani et ii. bordarii cum i. caruca et iiij. acris prati. Vetebrand tenet de rege. Valet v. solidos.

Interior of Melbourne Church – one of the finest and most complete
Norman churches in England

12

previously belonged to Alfgar, Earl of Mercia. Cox has it, but Stenton is less sure, that Alfgar had rebelled against King Edward, for which he was punished by having all these lands taken from him. They were given to his nephew Hugh who, like so many other knights, died fighting at Hastings. After the battle the two settlements of Aston and Weston became Crown property. After the re-allocation of land documented in the Domesday Survey, Aston remained divided in two manors.

One part remained with the Crown; the other and smaller part belonged to Henry de Ferrers. Shortly after the Domesday survey William passed the royal manor of Weston to his close friend Hugh d'Avranches, whom he had appointed Earl of Chester. Hugh was later to donate Weston to Chester's Abbey of St. Werburgh, his gift including the ferry over the Trent to Castle Donington and fishing rights on the river.

A few miles to the south, Bretby had also belonged to Alfgar but unlike Weston, had been bequeathed to Alfgar's son Edwin, who fell at Hastings. The holding then reverted to King William, who passed it to the Earl of Chester. Melbourne, a large manor that had belonged to King Edward was now William's estate, including at Domesday 24 acres of meadow and enough arable land to occupy six plough teams for a year. Further south still, the two manors of Walton-on-Trent and Rosliston, with their 40 acres of meadow, also belonged to the King.

King William's South Derbyshire territory, wedge-shaped, ran from Repton and Willington eastwards to Ticknall and Melbourne. To his victorious Norman knights he had granted huge tracts of the East Midlands. De Stafford was given much of the land below the middle Trent, between Burton and Ashby, including the exposed Coal Measures that underlay Gresley, Swadlincote and Newhall. These were covered by poor, cold, forested clays which gave way, past Castle Gresley, to the higher ground around Linton

where marl and drift together provided excellent ground for
cereals.

POSSESSIONS OF NIGEL DE STAFFORD
(with neighbouring religious houses)

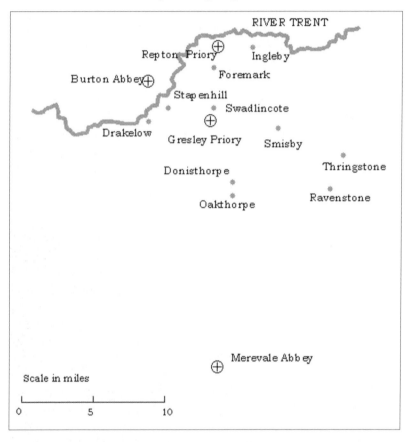

By far the greatest beneficiary however, in the South
Derbyshire area and further north, was Henry de Ferrers.
Many of these de Ferrers lands were then leased to others,
with Marston-on-Dove and Church Broughton given out-
right to the Priory of Tutbury in neighbouring Staffordshire.

Castle Knob, Church Gresley, site of the Norman castle

Drakelowe Hall, demolished in 1934.
Drakelow was owned by the Gresley family for 850 years

LAND IN SOUTH DERBYSHIRE
HELD BY HENRY DE FERRERS

Arleston	Hilton
Ash	Linton
Aston-on-Trent	Marston on Dove
Barrow-on-Trent	Osleston
Barton Blount	Sapperton
Bearwardcote	Scropton
Burnaston	Sinfin
Catton	Spondon
Chellaston	Stanton-by-Bridge
Church Broughton	Stenson
Cottons (on the edge of Sinfin Moor, in Normanton parish)	Stretton-en-le-Field
Croxall	Sudbury
Edingale	Sutton-on-the-Hill
Etwall	Swarkestone
Foston	Thurvaston
Hartshorne	Twyford
Hatton	Willesley

The bulk of the inhabitants of thinly-populated South Derbyshire were not great landowners but farming people of varying status: peasant proprietors (socmen), who elsewhere were known as freemen (liberi homines), bondsmen who held land on condition that they would provide military service for their lord and the more numerous villeins who, says Stenton, in later times were reckoned to be less than free,[3] but at Domesday had been merely 'villagers'. An idea of the numbers of socmen and villeins living in the area can be gained from an analysis of Derbyshire villages carried out by Paul Vinogradoff.

Vinogradoff's classification was an attempt to rank Derbyshire's settlements. According to his grading system a large village was one containing over 12 households, a small village of 6-11 households and a hamlet of 2-5 households. The working population he divided into villeins (serfs) and socmen (free citizens).[4]

DE STAFFORD LANDS IN SOUTH DERBYSHIRE
AT DOMESDAY AS CATEGORISED BY VINOGRADOFF
(Socman and Villein Holdings)[5] (The number of socman holdings is underlined)

Over 12 households
Lullitune	21	Lullington
Edunghale	16	Edingale
Stapenhille	16	Stapenhill
Wineshalle	6, 10	Winshill

6-11 households
Swardingscotes	1 cens,* 4	Swadlincote
Tichenhalle	2, 5	Ticknall
Engelebie	3, 4	Ingleby

2-5 households
Fernewerche	5	Foremark
Smidesbie	5	Smisby
Single householders		
Stantun	1	Stanton-by-Newhall

Complicated settlements
Drachelawe and Hedcote 6		Drakelowe and Heathcote

*cens. = censarius: a person paying tribute in money rather than service to his lord.

"Wasta" ('Waste' areas, with no inhabitants)
Achotorp, Durandestorp, Linctune, Rauenestun, Trangesby, (Oakthorpe, Donisthorpe, Linton, Ravenstone, Thringstone.)

Conditions for the English peasants did not change dramatically with the Conquest: old lords were exchanged for new, there was a continuity of work and debt, but now Norman instead of English lords were owed a series of duties and obligations. The Domesday Survey of 1086 concentrated the picture of rural society in which peasant farmers, in return for parcels of land, were required to perform labour service and provide a quantity of goods or money for their lord. Local circumstances would dictate the detail of transactions; for instance, in the Swadlincote area, an obligation or debt could be met by the delivery of so many carts of coal. In the Derwent valley north of Derby the survey reported the regular delivery to the lord of a quantity of honey. Some villeins held a large amount of land, but it was quality rather than acreage that mattered – and the Survey did not distinguish between good and indifferent soil, in recording land under the plough.

In Domesday terms, each 'plough' was the area covered in a year by a team of eight oxen. In the royal manor of Melbourne the king's own workforce operated a single plough, whilst twenty villeins and six bordars – each with a cottage – worked five ploughs. In 1086 Melbourne as a whole paid ten pounds in tax – as it did, said the Survey, in King Edward's time. These figures compare with the break-down of de Stafford lands where, on the four largest settlements – Lullington, Edingale, Stapenhill and Winshill – 92 per cent of the heads of household were villeins.[6] On the de Ferrers territory of Burnaston with Barrowcote, Henry's own men tilled land for three ploughs, whilst eight villeins and one bordar had four ploughs.

<h3 style="text-align:center">A RULING CLASS:</h3>
<h4 style="text-align:center">COMPETITION BETWEEN LOCAL LANDOWNERS</h4>

As land was redistributed after the Conquest, there was competition for ownership between lords and clergy, with peasants being beholden to one or other of them. South of the coalfield, Merevale Abbey had an interest in Hautboys

A fine Norman doorway, Melbourne Parish Church

Wood in the Seal area[7] but the canons of Gresley and William of Cauldwell were recorded as having been denied access to the Seal woods.[8] Because heath and waste were historically unkempt and uncultivated, there was a tendency for them to be both unfenced and open to dispute. Such land was unattended for long periods of the year and disputes were numerous along the Burton-Merevale-Coventry road, including the "rid of waste land in Norton Heath, near the road leading from Twycross to Clifton"[9] and later the "heath and waste of Sherwode in Overseale."[10]

At the furthest part of Derbyshire, Simon 'le Seler' of Seal leased to Merevale Abbey meadow near the Mease and three acres of arable land on Hopynges, Chichehul, Ruedych and Cliftunedych.[11] In Henry III's reign John Wyschard granted to Richard, son of Hugo Nechs, half a virgate of land in the (open) fields of Seal, along with a rood in Lathemedue, 'near to the Grey Monks' meadow'.[12] Today there is rich alluvium along the Mease and its Seal tributary and the remains of similar deposits that followed the floods at the end of the Ice Age.

The mixed wood and pasturelands were the scene of a two-stage negotiation between William de 'Wauere', Abbot of Merevale and Nicholas de Segrave. The Abbot first demanded access – 'common of pasture' – to the de Segrave woods in Grimeswood and Rosliston, via a road or track 'forty feet wide'[13] but in the same reign of Edward I, he gave up this access claim in return for four acres of the de Segrave wood in Le Hautboys in Seal.[14]

CONTROL FROM THE CENTRE

Though the structure of society and administration was little altered by the Norman Conquest, the English people had acquired masters speaking a different tongue. Through the shire and its officers inherited from their predecessors, Norman kings dispensed favours and justice. Patronage and redistribution of land were priorities for the king's men,

Henry de Ferrers being especially favoured with manors in central and southern Derbyshire. A descendant, Robert, was made Earl of Derby by King Stephen.

South of the Trent, the lands of de Stafford (later, Gresley) families were surrounded by the holdings of religious houses. The social structure of power was pyramidal: below the monarch and his counsellors were those newly endowed with lands and titles – alongside them, the clergy, natural allies of the king. Monarchy and Church were equally interested in the promotion of social order, any disturbance to which would bring upon an offender the heavy weight of the royal law. Within a wide definition of things spiritual the Church could arraign and punish malefactors, most of South Derbyshire falling within the diocese of Lichfield and Coventry. The king's law was administered within a county by the shire reeve or sheriff. At first Derbyshire had to manage with the services of a sheriff shared with Nottinghamshire: only from the 14th century did each of these counties have a sheriff to itself. By the end of Elizabeth's reign, four Gresleys had been Derbyshire sheriffs, as was Godfrey Thacker, in 1619, from Repton and Henry Harpur, in 1625 from Calke.

COUNTY SHERIFFS DRAWN FROM SOUTH DERBYSHIRE
1358 Johannes de Gresley
1426 Sir Thomas de Gresley
1453 Sir John Gresley, knight
1588 Thomas Gresley of Drakelow, Esq.
1616 Thomas Burdett of Foremark, Esq.
1619 Godfrey Thacker of Repton, Esq.
1625 Henry Harpur of Calke, Esq.

Cox records the contemporary citation of Henry Harpur ("a true-hearted Protestant") on his being elevated to a baronetcy in 1626 and then serving the Royalist cause; that he had "stood as an oak" against the Parliamentarians before sequestration of his property to the value of £578. 8s 2d.[15]

As with the office of sheriff, other elements of the administration of the law in Derbyshire were shared. Until the reign of Henry III, the assize for Derbyshire and Nottinghamshire was held entirely in Nottingham, which was also home for a gaol serving the two counties.[16]

A shift in power relationships came in the reign of Edward I, with two knights from each shire being commissioned to attend Parliament in Westminster. In 1295 Giles de Meynell thus attended for Derbyshire; in 1299, Geoffrey de Gresley and Robert de Frescheville. In 1324, for his attendance, Sir Hugh Meynell received 3s 4d per day, plus a journeying allowance. In other years, the daily rate varied between 4s and 5s per day, when presumably these knights and gentlemen at such rates, disbursed through the sheriff, would not have lost financially.[17]

THE GRESLEY FAMILY

The Gresleys were a family who could trace their origins back to the Norman Conquest. They were descended through the de Staffords, from the Norman de Toenis, one of the numerous Norman families who had taken up residence in England after the death of Harold. It was Nigel de Stafford whose possessions were tabulated in the great Domesday Survey. Some time between 1130 and 1151, William the son of Nigel changed his family name to Gresley.

The family owned extensive properties in southernmost Derbyshire and on the banks of the Trent. Church Gresley and Castle Gresley (founded a little later) were located mainly in the Gresley family's manor of Hedcote remembered today in the Hearthcote Road of Swadlincote.

They established their home at Drakelowe and stayed there for many generations. It was William de Gresley who founded the Priory and constituent church that were known after his family name.

SIR GEORGE GRESLEY'S FINANCIAL PROBLEMS.

Although they were major landowners the family had problems at times during their long history. Sir George Gresley suffered material losses during the civil war from his isolation as a Parliamentarian in a strongly royalist part of the Midlands. In 1660 he raised in Parliament the matter of the settlement that became urgent with the difficulties between himself and his wife.

"Arguments in favour of the bill of Sir George Gresley Bart., stating that Susan his wife brought him in marriage 2,000 l, that he settled 3,000 l, in trust to her, but eight years ago she left him taking with her 1,000 l, money in hand and many household goods, wherefore he desires that his lands be freed from a rent-charge of 55 l, a year, which was settled on her after his decease, and that no children born since the separation may be accounted his."
Endorsed: 'Sir George Gresley. Parliament'.[18]

THE HARPUR – CREWE DYNASTY

The Harpur family had for a long time been connected with the Middle Trent but Richard Harpur, who died in 1575, was the first of its members to live at Swarkestone, after marriage to Jane Findern brought to the Harpurs the manors of Findern and Swarkestone.

Richard Harpur of Swarkestone had land extending from Ticknall to Repton. His grandson Henry bought the manor of Calke in 1622 and his grandson, John, the third baronet eventually became heir to Swarkestone and Calke, becoming one of the largest landowners in the area. It was as master of Calke that Sir John's son, also named John, married Catherine, the youngest daughter and co-heiress of Lord Crewe of Steane in Northamptonshire. Sir John built the present house of Calke in the period between 1701 and 1703. In that age marriage provided the mechanism for the development of great estates and it was assumed that young women would accommodate themselves to the interests of property.

The outstanding member of the Crewe family – Sir George (1795-1844) was notable in an illiberal age for his progressive ideas on society. Sir George, himself the son of an atypical member of the line and a lady's maid, was a formidable champion of the farming interest. It was, he said, against his better inclination that he was persuaded to stand for Parliament, being elected as a Conservative for South Derbyshire in 1835. He was paternalistic in labour relations. Colin Kitching quotes Sir George's strong feelings on his own part in the parliamentary process: 'I hate Politics – because they involve all the Bitterness, the Rancour, the Prejudice of Party.'[19]

THE MEYNELLS, DETHICKS AND THEIR LANDS [20]

To the east of Burton-on-Trent, the manors of Newhall, Stanton Ward and Heathcote belonged to the family of de la Ward. In the reign of Edward I, Joan, daughter and heiress of Robert de la Ward, by marriage brought these manors and the advowson of Hartshorne into the regionally significant family of Meynell. There were no sons from the marriage, but John, son of Sir William Dethick, married the heiress of this branch of the Meynells and for seven generations Dethicks continued as landowners in Newhall. Humphrey Dethick died in 1599 and his sons were without issue. The Dethick property including the rectory of Hartshorne passed to Humphrey's daughter Katherine, who married Alexander Redishe.

The family of Meynell bought the former Gresley priory lands in 1728, selling them on in 1775 to the Gresleys (the Priory's original founders).

Powerful as these great landowning families were, no one was above the law and, locally, disputes between both lords of the manor or others of the landed gentry and

24

religious houses would be settled by a jury, summoned by the sheriff and composed of other men of property from Derbyshire or neighbouring counties. Duties extended throughout society and were enforceable by law: thus, all who lived from the land were beholden to the Church, their spiritual overload, to whom were due regular tithes – an onerous burden, payable within each parish – and from each producer, great or small.

1 Stenton, F.M., Anglo-Saxon England, Oxford University Press: Oxford, c. 1971, p. 658.
2 Ibid., p. 672.
3 Stenton, op. cit., p. 477.
4 Vinogradoff, Paul, English Society in the 11th Century, Oxford University Press, 1908, p. 270.
5 Vinogradoff op. cit., (Appendix V), p. 495.
6 Page, W., Victoria History of the County of Derbyshire [henceforward VCH], 2 vols., London, 1905, Vol. II, Domesday Survey, (The holders of lands), p. 345.
7 Jeayes Charter no. 159 (c. 1300): Charters and Muniments of the Marquis of Anglesey, William Salt Archive Society, Stafford.
8 Rydeware Charter no. 18, Edward II vol. XVI (1325), John Rylands Library, Manchester.
9 Jeayes Charter no. 162 (14th century), op. cit.
10 Ibid., no. 173 (14th century).
11 Ibid., no. 75, dated 9 April 1247.
12 Ibid., no. 97.
13 Ibid., no. 129, dated 1284.
14 Ibid., no. 159.
15 Cox, John Charles, Three Centuries of Derbyshire Annals, Vol. 2, Bemrose & Sons: London & Derby, 1890, pp. 37-9.
16 VCH. Vol. II, p. 95.
17 Ibid., p. 98.
18 State Papers, Domestic Series. Charles II., 1660-61, British Library, pp. 457-8.
19 Kitching, Colin (ed.), Squire of Calke Abbey: Extracts from the journals of Sir George Crewe of Calke Abbey, South Derbyshire, 1815-1834, Scarthin: Cromford, 1995, p. 12.
20 Cox, op. cit. Churches of Derbys., Vol. 1, p. 329.

CHAPTER 3

THE RELIGIOUS HOUSES

THE PRIORY OF REPTON

Repton Priory was founded in the 12th century by Maud (also known as Matilda), daughter of the Earl of Gloucester (a natural son of Henry I). Maud was the widow of Ralph Gurnon, 4th Earl of Chester. Canons from Calke were sent to establish the new priory.[1]

Among early bequests to Repton was a major endowment in 1285 by William and Roger de Hartshorne of 125 acres of land and wood in Hartshorne, and this was followed in 1290 by a bequest at Ingleby of three virgates and a bovate of arable land, eight acres of meadow and five acres of woodland. Also in Edward II's reign, Harold de Leke assigned to the priory for one day in every year the labour of sixty serfs on his land at Staunton Harold.[2]

The Augustinian canons of Repton performed the functions of parish priests in the villages of Foremark, Ingleby, Newton Solney, Bretby, Ticknall, Measham and Smisby – most of these, de Stafford lands. The Priory's reputation was tested during a visitation by the Bishop of Lichfield on 2 November 1364. Business talk in the chapter house between Bishop and Prior was rudely interrupted by a shower of arrows fired by a mob of local peasants, some penetrating the narrow windows. The precise reason for the assault is not known and it was brought to an end with the Bishop rescued only by the arrival of a force of armed retainers despatched to Repton by Sir Alaric de Solney (Newton Solney) and Robert Francis (Foremark). The siege had lasted 14 hours. When the Bishop reached Lichfield, he pronounced a sentence of "grave excommunication" on all who had taken part in the affray.[3]

Priors of Repton[4]

Robert	1153-60
Nicholas	1172-81
Albred	c1200
Richard	1208
Nicholas	c1215
John	1220
Reginald	c1230
Peter	1252
Richard	1268
Robert	1289
Ralph	1316-36
John de Lichfield	1336-46
Simon de Sutton	1346-56
Ralph Derby	1356-99
William of Tutbury	1399
William Maynesin	c1411
Wystan Porter resigned 'due to old age and infirmity' (VCH)	1436
John Overton	1436-38
John Wylne	1438-71
Thomas Sutton	1471-86
Henry Prest	1486-1503
William Derby	1503-08
John Young (died before completion of surrender)	1508

The Common
Seal of Repton
Priory

Gresley Priory

Gresley's priory started like Repton's in the 12th century, but had only four canons – a small foundation in comparison with many of the 42 other Augustinian (Austin) houses. The foundation is variously placed in the reign of Henry I (Dugdale) or Stephen (Dom. Knowles).

The black canons, so called after the colour of their robes, filled at Gresley the role of both monk and parish priest,

27

holding services in priory and church. A church, dedicated eventually to both St. George and St. Mary, was an integral part of the monastic buildings, the nave being used by parishioners and the choir or chancel by the canons, for whom it was their priory chapel.[5] All Gresley priors would be expected to spend some time on the house's estates that extended south and east of the Trent, abutting on properties of other religious houses. Eventually in an area where good arable land was at a premium there were bound to be long-running issues of ownership and access.

Gresley's first prior, Reginald, was named in a 12th century agreement that concerned Lullington[6] and had as one of its witnesses the priory's Brother Gilbert. In 1268, the confirmation charter issued to the priory by Geoffrey de Gresley detailed the extensive properties of the priory, extending from Church Gresley to Linton and from there towards Caldwell. They included meadows, arable and woodland, mills and ponds, giving a picture of variety and good farming practice.

In 1341, Brother Henry de Bently became vicar of Lullington and at the same time there was an increase in the total of Gresley brothers from four to six made possible by

Smisby Church in 1790. The oldest part, the south aisle, was built by the Repton monks in 1068

the receipt of the extra income from Lullington. A very short time afterwards, Prior Roger de Aston fell victim to the Black Death that had already struck the city of Derby.

PRIORS OF GRESLEY[7]

Reginald Shirley		1151-57
Walter		c1200
Reginald		c1200
Richard I		c1240
Henry		1252
Richard II	died	1281
William de Seyle		1281
Robert de Gresley		1308
Roger de Aston	(died of the plague)	1311-48
John Walrant		1349
John Gresley		1360-61
John Hethcote	died	1400
John Tutbury	appointed	1400
Simon Balsham		1420
William of St. Yvo	died	1438
Richard of Coventry	appointed	1438
Thomas		1450
John Smyth	died	1493
Robert Mogge	appointed	1493
John Okeley	surrendered the priory	1536-43

There are firm starting and leaving dates for only three priors besides Reginald, the first occupant: Roger de Aston, John Gresley and the last prior – John Okeley. The three priors – Walter, Reginald and Richard I – in the first half of the 13th century are allotted the approximate dates given them in the Victoria County History.

Control of the priory was exercised through its own Augustinian Order, a decree by the Lateran Council in 1215 having laid down that all houses were to be visited by 'wise persons',[8] responsible to the Pope. Triennial Chapters of the

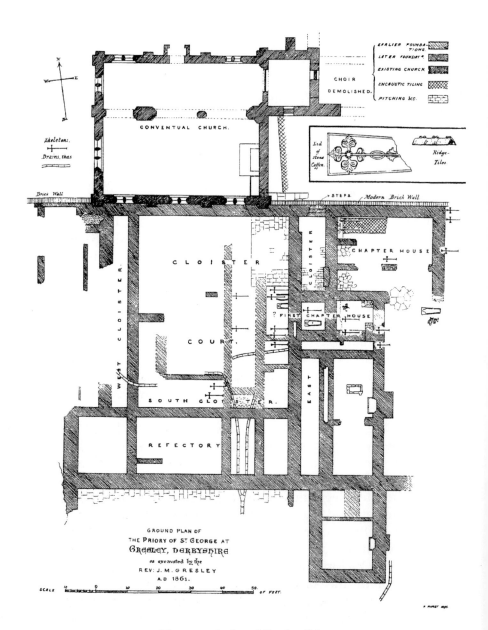

The ground plan of Gresley Priory

Common seal of Gresley Priory

Order were held. The houses often failed to send a representative for which they could be punished by a fine. In 1509, 28 houses were un-represented at the Chapter held at Leicester, when the Prior of Gresley was fined 6s 8d[9] for non-attendance and failure to send a proctor in his place. It was not the visitation of the Order but of the bishop which was respected most[10] and his enquiries could be most meticulous.[11]

GRESLEY CHURCH AND PRIORY – CONFIRMATION CHARTER, 1268 (TRANSLATION EXTRACT)

To all Christians who will see or hear (this present) writing, Geoffrey de Gresel, son and heir of master William de Gresel, health (in the Lord) everlasting. Know ye all that I have seen, admitted and fully understood charters and confirmations made and granted by my predecessors of God and blessed Mary and the church of Saint George of Gresel, and the canons there who will serve God for ever, concerning many and divers land and tenements and liberties; that is by master William de Gresel, son of Geoffrey de Gresel, my grandfather, whereby he gave to the aforesaid church and canons in pure and perpetual alms, free and quiet from all secular service, four acres of land which Stephen P (... held, with messuages) and all other appurtenances, and he gave in addition to the same in the aforesaid manner the wood and field that he acquired by agreement from Robert de Sogunhul and Petronilla, [his] wife (... extending) from Bucks putte syche and Merneya as far as the boundary between the said William and the aforesaid Robert. Likewise of the aforesaid Geoffrey, my grandfather, whereby he gave to the same two pieces of cultivated land (…) lying between the way which leads from Gresel to the gate of this park, and two acres which the aforesaid canons previously held his gift in the same cultivated land (…way… Linton) and hayam from the park towards Chyrche Gresel on each side of the stream which goes out of his park of Gresel. He gave also to the same two acres of land which lie (…Wy…) of William Scot, his uncle, in pure and perpetual alms, free and quiet from all secular service. He gave also to the same in the aforesaid manner all that land which is between Nov (…) of the canons, that is the ditch which begins at Brechia which was of John, son of Walter, and extends in length as far as the spring by the halle stude, as so descending (as far as …) Cowehurst and from Cowehurst as far as the Scotces flat, as so ascending as far as the garden which master William de Gresel gave to the aforesaid canons. He gave also to the same (…) land which Ralph the smith and William, his son, held of the same in Chyrche Gresel, that is in pure and perpetual alms, free and quiet and peaceful from all secular service pertaining to him and his heirs. He gave also to the same a certain garden which was once of William le Scot, through the external ditch which is towards Caldewallhul and so the old ditch extends in a circuit with one fishpond, and the whole land is within the close, wholly in pure and perpetual alms, free and quiet, peaceful and whole, as any alms free and good can be given to have and hold. He gave also to the same all the cultivated land lying between the plain of Heccote and Le wommoune lon des, which is called Prustes Buttes, and a half acre of land under Chadelowe extending towards Heccote, and eight furrowe lying in the cultivated land which is called Benche Brede furlong, in pure and perpetual alms, free and quiet, peaceful and discharged from all secular service and demand belonging to me and my heirs. He gave also the same a toft that William Scotticus, his uncle, held in the vill of Castel Gresel, that is

32

the one which lies between the cultivated land which was of the same William and the fishpond of the same, and between the path which goes from the fishpond in Gresel to the fishpond of the said William, as the old dich shows, with a meadow which lies between the arable field Peseberwe Syche and the head of the way which leads from Linton at Gresel and in addition the meadow which lies between the way which goes from Linton at Gresel and Caldewall hul and between the boundaries of the meadow of Linton and Peseberwe Syche, in pure and perpetual alms free and quiet from all secular service and extraction belonging to him or his heirs. Likewise of master William, son of Geoffrey de Gresel, my father, who gave to the same the mill of Castel Gresel with all appurtenances....

These being witnesses; master John, then Abbot of Burton, master Richard, then Prior of Repton, John Grym, Ralph de la Lache, William de Meysham, William de Herteshorn, Rodger de (...) renham, Milo de Menter, William de Rol Weston, William Grym, Randolph Oky and others. Done at Gresel on the morrow of Saint James the apostle 26 July in the sixty-eighth year of my indulgence (?). 52 Henry III (added in later hand – 17th Century).

Original held at Henry E. Huntington Library & Art Gallery, San Marino, California, USA

GRESLEY LANDS

In the year 1268 Geoffrey de Gresley, a member of the family that had founded the church of St. George and its associated priory, signed a charter confirming gifts to them. Among the charter's witnesses were John the Abbot of Burton and Richard the Prior of Repton: they testified to the lands, properties and possessions given by Geoffrey to the church and the priory of Austin canons. The gifts included a wood and field originally belonging to Robert de Sogunhul and his wife Petronilla, whilst another source recorded the

Seal of Richard, Prior of Gresley
c.1250

same married couple as having bequeathed to Burton Abbey the rent from a Swadlincote property.

The Gresley confirmation charter is of special interest to researchers in having identified in Geoffrey's gift the names of fields and other farmland. Most of the field names quoted for 1268 were to reappear some 270 years later in the bailiff's inventory of priory possessions produced after Henry VIII's dissolution of the religious houses.

Fields that were named in both 1268 and 1536 were: Cowhurst and Scotts Flat in the Castle Gresley area, Priests Butts near to Cadley Hill and Peasbarrow in the neighbourhood of Swain's Park. Two field names recorded in 1268 but missing at the later date were Benchebrede and Guguriwetoft, near Linton.

A Patent Roll of 1363[12] gives the dimensions of holdings that were not part of the priory's land: seven acres of (arable) land; five acres of meadow and five acres of wood belonging to John Woodward in Hethcote, Swadlincote and Church Gresley; six acres of (arable) land and one rood of meadow belonging to William Francis; and seven acres of arable land and one rood of meadow belonging to 'Henry son of Ralph'.

On the other hand, between Hearthcote and Stapenhill, we find in 1404 that Thomas Southam had held 35 acres of meadow as against fifteen acres of arable.[13]

The most illuminating evidence of land utilisation in the area is contained in the Bailiff's Accounts of 1536 for the former Gresley Priory estate:

WOODLAND	Acreage
Burnley Wood	16
	16
MEADOW	
Wheteclose	34
Gostcrofts	10
Thrumlowe Close	$6^{1}/2$
Syslowe Close	18
Hallows Close	8
Cowclose	10
Scotts Meadow	4
Tubbe Meadow	$2^{1}/2$
Tithemede	3
Horgetmede	1
Cawsymede	1
Pesebarre	3
Brome Meadow	3
	104
ARABLE	
Wheteclose	6
Fellowfield	4
Almeclose	$3^{1}/2$
Prysts Butts	4
Crabtreflat	$2^{1}/2$
Pesebarowe	3
Crosseflatte	$2^{1}/2$
	$25^{1}/2$[xiv]

Statistics for the neighbouring manor of Swadlincote in Elizabeth's reign had clearly been consolidated: they were for 300 acres of (arable) land, 100 acres of meadow, 200 acres of pasture, 100 acres of wood and 100 acres of 'furze and heath'. Presumably the purchaser, John Breton of Worthington, Leicestershire, was interested less in the size of these plots than in their valuation: in 1567 they cost him £100.[15]

A similar document for the same land two years later showed a different breakdown: 200 acres of arable, 20 acres of meadow, 100 acres of pasture and 20 acres of woodland.[16]

When Sir Christopher Alleyn of Gresley was attainted of High Treason we have the benefit of the inventory made of the 'corne and cattell' 52 acres of wheat, 18 acres of oats and seven acres of peas. In addition, out of corn gathered and threshed or waiting to be threshed, valuation showed the wheat to have been worth nearly twice as much as the barley per quarter: 22s as against 12s:[17] prices that were much less than those quoted elsewhere in Derbyshire.[18]

Sir Christopher's cattle were itemised with their value:

		£	s.	d.
Drawing oxen	8	30.	0.	0.
Plough Horses	2	5.	0.	0.
Kyne	14	32.	13.	4.
Heyfers	2	4.	0.	0.
Yearinges	12	6.	12.	0.

In business terms the religious houses were of great regional significance – able to argue a case on the basis of at least equality with other considerable landowners, including members of titled families. The land in the lower part of South Derbyshire, variable in quality, contained good soil to the west of Linton, and was competition elsewhere for timber and solid fuel.

A 14th century charter refers to a typical dispute of access and usage between the Gresley Prior on the one hand and, on the other, John Grym and Robert de Findern. Mostly waste ground within the vill of Swadlincote, the land in question adjoined a wood that it was agreed belonged to the priory. The dispute was settled in this form:

"That the aforesaid prior and Convent and their successors shall henceforth have the tenor of their charter which they have of the aforesaid William, so that they may approw it at their own will, without disturbance from the aforesaid J. and R. and their heirs, save that the piece of ground be common in open time and that they allow a road from that side towards the Whiteleyes leading from the aforesaid wood to .... Hethcote, of the breadth of forty feet."[19]

Witn: Willian de Ingewardeby, Ralph de Irland, William de Saperton, Thomas de Mackeleye, John Oky, Nicholas de le Sale, Adam Thurmot, and others. Written at Gresley, the Tuesday in Easter week in the twelfth year of the reign of King Edward II (1319)

It was customary in the Middle Ages, in making a will, to leave a tenth of an estate 'for the good of one's soul' to the incumbent of the parish church.[20] It was in this spirit that a knighted member of the Gresley family obtained a licence to alienate substantial properties in the Gresley/Swadlincote area to the priory and church. (Alienation involved evasion of the obligations that the Statute of Mortmain laid on beneficiaries of a will. According to this, all lands were assumed to belong to the king who rented them out to his nobles in exchange for military service by them and their retainers.)

37 Edward III
May 8, Westminster.
Licence for the alienation in mortmain by John de Greselye, knt to the Prior and Convent of the Church of St. George, Greselye, in satisfaction of 20s. of £10 yearly of land and rent, which they have (found) the king's licence to acquire of a messuage, a virgate of land, 5 acres of meadow, 5 acres of wood and a rent of 1 lb of pepper and 1 lb of cumin, in Hathcote, Swarthingcote and Churchegreseleye, and of the reversions of a messuage, 6 acres of land and 1 rood of meadow held by William Fraunceys; 2 messuages, 7 acres

of land and 1 rood of meadow there, held by Henry, son of Ralph; a messuage, 3 acres of land and 1 rood of meadow there, held for life by Thomas Balle; a messuage and virgate of land in Swartlingcote, held for life by John Anneys; a messuage, a virgate of land and 1 rood of meadow in the same town, held for life by Agnes de Cesteford; and 1 acre of land in Swartlingcote, held for life by Thomas de Walton; all which tenements are held for others than the king; and one of the value of the 10s yearly; as has been found by inquisition taken by Philip de Lutteleye, escheator to the county of Derby.[21]

A substantial part of the priory's income was from mortuary fees, fines and tithes. The de Fyndern family, as a reward for the work involved in fencing their wood in Swadlincote, were excused for three years (1414-17) from tithes payable to the Priory (Phillips No. 326), but royal treasurers became increasingly restive about the amount of potential revenue lost to the Crown by alienation.

In 1313, a dispute between Merevale Abbey, Warwickshire, and Thomas de Rideware was settled by a covenant: Thomas released to the Abbey "all claim to common of pasture in the heath and waste of Sherwood in Overseale."[22] At this period not all disputes were settled so peacefully. Under Edward II, who came to the throne in 1307, nobles changed sides and kings were insecure. Opponents of the Crown were strong in Derbyshire and Edward's allies, attempting to seize the bridge at Burton, were repulsed there. Instead they forded the Trent at Walton and proceeded to lay waste to whatever belonged to the king's enemies in the southern half of Derbyshire.[23]

BURTON ABBEY AND ITS DERBYSHIRE CONNECTIONS
Burton Abbey was responsible for churches in Derbyshire as well as Staffordshire. In the typical stone-built monastic edifice, a community would congregate at least once a week

for prayer and in addition the Abbey would be expected to give both hospitality and shelter to the deserving and well intentioned. At the Staffordshire end of a bridge from Derbyshire, the house had spacious guest quarters that were accustomed to receiving important visitors, including royalty.

Of the two houses, Burton Abbey and Gresley Priory, Burton's was much the earlier foundation, having been founded before the Conquest in the period 1002-4 by Wulfric, Earl of Mercia, who gave to the abbey all his paternal inheritance, a bequest that included, in Derbyshire, Winshill, Sutton-on-the-Hill, Ticknall and Breadsall.[24] Derbyshire at that period included Appleby, where it was recorded by the Domesday Survey:

'In Applebi the abbot of Burton had five carucates of land to be taxed. Land to five ploughs. Leuric the abbot made over one carucate of this land to countess Govida, which the king now has'.[25]

East of Burton and south of the Trent were the Derbyshire holdings of Burton Abbey, a 15th century charter listing one group of these:

34 acres of arable land and one piece of meadow (Caldlewesich) in Hethcote;
2 messuages, 2 virgates of arable and an acre of meadow called Kirkmeadow in Stapenhill;
a further 15 acres – not itemised.[26]

A King's writ on 26 August, in the fifth year of Henry IV's reign, granted all of these lands to Henry Bradfield 'for his good services'. It was on such grounds that a substantial part of the property of the whole kingdom had been acquired. On the death of the said Henry Bradfield, another writ was issued to the sheriff of the county of Derby enquiring into these lands held ultimately from the Crown and – perhaps a surprising statement:

> 'which the Abbot and Convent of Burton by special license of the King acquired – in order to ascertain on what day the said Henry died, who were and are the occupiers of the said lands, the value of them, etc., and meanwhile to seize the said lands.'[27]

Much territory, at the Conquest, had been given to Norman knights in recognition of services rendered to the Crown, but there was concern on all sides that shrewd businessmen-abbots were greatly enlarging their holdings in processes that would require a royal fiat to nullify.

Burton was a moderately large house, under Abbot Laurence (1229-60), with 30 monks, compared with the modest complement (4-6) at Gresley. From Derbyshire, Burton was bequeathed the rent from two bovates in Swadlincote,[28] Robert of Sugkenhull and his wife Petronilla having given up their claim to the sixpenny annual sum due from the land.

The religious houses, as major landowners, were able to bargain with the most powerful members of the local community. A significant charter from the latter part of the 14th century covers the litigation (Abbot of Burton against Sir Thomas Gresley) relating to the rich pasture alongside the Trent. A sub-plot relates to the work that a feudal lord could demand of peasant farmers, and the theme of access to common grazing begun long before these incidents and continued for many generations after.

Memorandum laid by the Abbot of Burton against Sir Thomas de Gresley[29] (main charges – translation)
Charges:
i) That Sir Thomas, after "the carrying of the hay from New Meadow in the twentieth year of the reign of King Richard II

in which the abbot and his community had enclosed" the field.
ii) That Sir Thomas "claims from the cottars of Caldwall, from every tenant that is, one day's work harvesting."
iii) That Sir Thomas "enclosed one meadow called Drakelow meadow and holds that field at all times of the year where it used to be at the disposal of the said abbot after hay-making."

An abbot could feel powerful enough to act without regard to niceties of procedure. In the early 15th century, it was reported that Burton's abbot had acquired 'without the king's license' a very substantial (34 acres) of land in Stapenhill and meadow in Hethcote. At the climax to its visitation by Cromwell's inquisitors, Burton was saved from the general dismemberment carried on in the region. After being surrendered to Thomas Legh by William Edys, the last abbot, on 14 November 1539, the Abbey in 1541 became the Collegiate Church of Burton with the former abbot as its incumbent, accompanied by possibly four of his monks.[30]

Henry Hastings, from his Leicestershire seat, had written to Cromwell, pointing out in his letter that Burton Abbey lay 'very convenient' to him – adding piquantly that he would have written earlier on the matter but for an attack of measles.[31]

1 VCH Vol. II, pp. 59-60.
2 Ibid.
3 Kitching, op. cit., m.s.
4 VCH Vol. II, p. 61.
5 Cox, op. cit. Churches of Derbys., Vol III; Hull, Oswald, Gresley – The Family, lands and Priory, Derbyshire Archaeological and Natural History Society, 1959, pp. 16-17.
6 Ibid, Hull, p. 14.
7 Sources: VCH, Derbys., vol. II, pp. 57-8; Madan, Falconer, The Gresleys of Drakelow: An account of the family, Oxford, 1899; Spavold, Janet (ed.), In the name of God, amen: Everyday life in South Derbyshire, 1535-1700, South Derbyshire Local History Research Group: Ashby de la

Zouch, c. 1992.

8 Salter, Rev. H.E. (ed.), Chapters of the Augustinian Canons, London, 1922, Intro. p. ix.

9 Ibid.

10 Ibid., p. xiii

11 Cheney, C.R., Episcopal visitation of monasteries in the thirteenth century, Manchester University Press, 1983. See also: Hull, Oswald, Gresley – The Family, lands and Priory, Derbyshire Archaeological and Natural History Society, 1959.

12 Pat. Roll 37 Edw. III (1363), British Library.

13 Jeayes Charter Nos. 614-615; 5 Henry IV (1404).

14 Derbyshire Deeds No. 2620, Account of William Cook, Bailiff, 27, 28 and 29 Henry VIII (1536-1538), Derbyshire Record Office.

15 Phillipps Charters Nos. 330-331 (9 Eliz.1), originals held by John Rylands Library, Manchester.

16 Phillipps Charter, op. cit., No. 334 (11 Eliz.1) 1569.

17 National Arhives, Kew, Surrey [henceforward TNA (PRO)] E/178/618 Mem.4. 29-31 Eliz. 1.

18 VCH Vol. II., p. 180. Wheat per quarter 54/8 (1622), barley per quarter 32/- (1622).

19 Phillipps Charter, op. cit., No. 312.

20 Spavold, op. cit., p. 201.

21 TNA (PRO) Pat. Roll 37 Edw. III. (M.19) dated 1363

22 Jeayes Charter no. 173.

23 Glover, Stephen, The History of the County of Derby, 2 vols., H. Mozley & Son: Derby, 1829, pp. 427-8.

24 VCH Staffs., Vol. 3, p. 199.

25 Glover, op. cit., Vol. 2, p. 23.

26 Jeayes Charter, op. cit., No. 616.

27 Ibid., No 678, dated 1441.

28 Jeayes Charter No. 66.

29 Ibid., No. 363 Temp. Ric. II.

30 VCH. Staffs., Vol. III, p. 210.

31 Ibid.

CHAPTER 4

DISSOLUTION

There had always been a special relationship in England between Church and Crown. England's King Henry VIII clung to the royal privilege of appointing the upper clergy but in 1534 he went much further, with the Act of Supremacy, that confirmed him as head of an Anglican state church. There followed threats, open or implied, from king and courtiers to religious houses whose wealth mocked the monarch's empty coffers.

The First Fruits, Tenths and Subsidy legislation of 1534 demanded "an increase and augmentation to be made for maintenance of his (the king's) most royal estate and for the defence of the realm", to be attained by "taking away the excess which is the great cause of the abuse of the Church".[1] It became clear that these edicts could produce investigation within this region of houses such as Repton, Gresley and the Abbey of Burton. Repton (income £180) came within the Act of Dissolution (1536) which said that, with an annual income below £200, a house would risk an adverse report by a royal agent, leading to possible dissolution.

AGENTS AND INVESTIGATORS

The two redoubtable investigators heading the northern visitations were men well chosen for their role: there was a high theological background to both Thomas Legh, DCL (responsible for the Derbyshire inquisition) and Thomas Layton, LLD, Clerk to the Council of the Chancery. The picture emerging from the letters of John Ap Rice[2] to their master, Thomas Cromwell is of men driven largely by personal aggrandisement and enrichment, with a targeted man being expected to offer an inducement. According to ap Rice, Legh was "young and of intolerable elation and excessive in talking", who handled abbots "very roughly". Investigators were encouraged by Cromwell to inform on each other.

The investigators were instructed to seek evidence of the use in churches of false images and to uncover details of excessively high living by abbots. The strong impression is that those accused had been found guilty ahead of the sifting of evidence, but one has to acknowledge that there was sufficient support for action against greedy heads of houses from both the public and, more importantly, their master Cromwell, to ensure the investigators' survival.

So long as the bill of charges against abbots and monks continued to accumulate in Cromwell's lap, the investigators were probably safe from retribution. There was widespread acceptance that abbots and monks had found difficulty in living up to their vows of chastity. Further, there could be pleaded justification for the exposure of deceptive practices: the use of 'relics' displayed as having come from the crucifixion or having been connected with the lives of the apostles and saints, and the display of what purported to be "a portion of the Cross" along with "the sword with which St. Thomas of Canterbury was martyred." From this distance in time one can say that the investigators, having searched for wrongdoing, had found it.

Legh, having passed into Derbyshire in October 1538, had secured the submission within four days of Darley, Dale and Repton. Repton's final surrender to Legh came three days after the death of Prior Young, and after the Crown's initial willingness to accept a large fine in lieu of dissolution. Thomas Thacker, who had been put in temporary possession for the process of dissolution, did very well from the purchase of Repton priory's fittings and contents.

Dr. Legh: The bill of charges[3]
Blitheman, cashier for the visitation, writes to Thomas Cromwell, forwarding Legh's damning report:

Repton Priory from the south west

27 HENRY VIII.   28 Feb. [1536].
363. WILLIAM BLITHMANNE to CROMWELL.
After the conclusion of the visitation for the King in the province of York has made a clean book of the compertes, which he sends by Cromwell's commissaries, Dr. Layton and Dr. Lee. Will bring a duplicate shortly himself. Parted from the commissaries at Ludlow, and returned to York for receipt of the first payment and sureties for the first-fruits of the monastery of Funtance, and other money due to the King, with which he will repair to London in the second week of Lent. Hopes to bring some acceptable commodity for his mastership. Ludlow, 28 Feb.
Hol., p.1. Add.: Master Thomas (Cr)umwell, secretary (pri)ncipal to the King's highness. Endd.: John Blitheman.

364. VISITATION OF MONASTERIES.
"Compendium compertorum per Doctorem Layton et Doctorem Legh, in visitatione regia in provincia Eboracensi ac episcopatu Coven. et Lichfelden."

<u>Monastery of Repyngdon alias Repton</u> – Thomas Rede, sub-prior, and three others, named as sodomites <u>per voluntarias pollutiones.</u>* Superstition: <u>A pilgrimage is made to St. Guthlac</u> and his bell, which they put upon people' heads to alleviate headache. Nicholas Page seeks to be released from religion. The house owes 100mks. Founder, the King.

<u>Grenesley</u>* – Founder, Sir George Grenesley. Annual rent, 40l.

<u>Cell of St. James Darby</u> – Thomas Gaynsborough, prior, guilty of incontinence with one single woman and one married woman. Founder, the King. Rents, 10l.

<u>Nuns of St. Mary Darby</u> – Superstition: they have part of the shirt of St. Thomas, which is reverenced among pregnant women. Founder, the King. Rents, 10l; debt, 20 mks.

<u>Dale</u> – Incontinence, John Staunton, abbot, with one single and one married woman; Wm. Bramston, with 5 married women. They reverence part of the girdle and the milk of St. Mary, and the wheel of St. Katharine in silver. Founder, Gervays Kyngeston. Rents, 140l.

* in consenting acts   Grenesley = Gresley

Examining the population of the priory, we see that changes to the personnel were slow, canons having tended to keep their posts for a long time, if not for life. But after the visitation to Repton by Cromwell's agent Legh, all was different. In his report, Legh named Thomas Rede, Thomas Dawes and Thomas Leycestre as sodomites. The priory, though liable to be dissolved, was granted exemption from that fate on 12 June 1537, paying an exorbitant fine of £266 13s 4d,1 but was forced finally to surrender on 25 October 1538: Prior Young had died less than a week before. On the day of surrender there were absent from the personnel Rede, Dawes and Lycestre, along with the long-serving Nicholas Page, who had asked to be released from his vows. The four leavers were to forfeit their pensions.

REPTON PRIORY – INDIVIDUALS IN A PERIOD OF TURMOIL [4]

	1496	1518	1521	1524	25.10.1538
prior	Henry Preiste	John Yong (1513)	John Yonge	John Young	vacant
sub	John Stewne	Richard Hough(1503)	Richard Houghe	Richard Hough	Ralph Clarke
	Richard Burton				
	Thomas Dawes	Thomas Dawes	Thomas Dawys	Thomas Dawys	
	Richard Clerke	Richard Murdacke	Richard Murdacke		
	John Wilford	Thomas Leycestre	Thomas Leycestre	Thomas Leycestre	
	William Devy	Thomas Gorton	Thomas Gorton	Thomas Gorton (curate of Bretby)	
	William Tutbury	Thomas Rede	Thomas Rede	Thomas Rede	
	Henry Belton	James Yonge	James Yonge	James Yonge	James Yonge
	John Rolton	John Asheby	John Asheby	John Asheby	John Asheby
	John Hynter	Thomas Pratt	Thomas Pratt	Thomas Pratt	Thomas Pratt
	William Machyn	Thomas Stringer (nov.)	Thomas Strynger	Thomas Stringer	Thomas Stringer
	Richard Murdack	Thomas Webster (nov.)	Thomas Webster (prof.nov.)	Thomas Wesbster	Thomas Webster
	John Wirksworth (nov.)	John Wirksworth	John Wyrkesworth	John Wirksworth (sacrist)	
	Richard Newhall (nov.)	Nicholas Page (nov.)	Nocholas Page (prof. nov.)	Nicholas Page	
				Robert Ward	Thos. Cordall
				John Kynton	Thomas Braunston
				Ralph Nyche	prof. Novices

(Spelling of surnames varies according to the preference of the clerk drawing up each roll)

A model of the Augustinian Priory of Repton which stood from 1172 until it was suppressed in 1538

REPTON PRIORY – PENSION PROVISIONS

Unless stated otherwise, the canons below signed the deed of surrender. Canons who were in residence at the time of the dissolution received an immediate award and a pension for life. Those who already served cures, as at Bretby, retained their benefices but did not receive a pension.

Pension   Status at surrender[5]

	£	s	d	
Ralph Clark	6			Sub prior Pension still claimed in 1558, but chaplain at Newton Solney in 1560
James Young	5	6	8	Canon
John Ashby	5			ditto
Thomas Pratt	5			do In 1553, held the cure of Bretby, a chapelry of Repton.
Thomas Stringer	5	6	8	Canon
Thomas Webster	5			ditto
Robert Ward	4			Novice
Thomas Braunston	4			ditto Did not sign deed of surrender.
John Smythe	2			Non canon, but received this sum as annuity.
Richard Hay	2			Non canon, but received this sum as annuity.
John Wirksworth	*			Claimed a pension but did not receive it as he held the benefice at Repton.
Thomas Cordall	2	16	8	Not recorded as a canon before the surrender.

Sums realised for goods and fittings sold (selected items only identified):

	£	s	d
The church. Alabaster and other tables.			
Images of St. Nicholas and of Our Lady		50	
Vestry. Albs and velvet copes. Cross in copper			
Other Vestments	4		
Cloisters		20	
Dorter. Contents of the cells		20	
Frater. Items include five tables		6	
Hall		2	
Buttery. Cupboards, chests and contents			
Including cloths, napkins and towels		10	
Prior's house. Furniture and covers		30	
Other rooms. Furniture and furnishings, including bedding			
The inner chamber		2	
The garden chamber		15	
The next chamber		20	
The hall chamber		10	
The high chamber			
The kitchen. 5 brass pots 2 spitts and other items		40	
The larder. Dripping pan, frying pan, grill, skimmer			
And other utensils		8	
Bruhouse. 2 bruing leadda, 1 mash fatte, tubs, cowls, 2 skippes		66	
The yelyghouse. 16 kelying leads, 2 mash fatts		40	
The boulting house. 2 hoffs, 1 boulting huch		20	
The kyllhouse. Heyr upon the kyll, sestiron of lead		26	8

Grain

	Shillings a quarter	£	S	d
1 quarter of wheat	8		8	
2 quarter of rye	7		14	
15 quarter of barley	4		60	
4 quarter of malt	5		20	

REPTON PRIORY: POST-DISSOLUTION SALE (CONT.)

6 quarter of pease	4	24
10 lodes of hay	2 & 8 pence	26 8
3 kye (20s), 10 horfays and 2 culde cartes	4	
1 reke of pease	7	

Total received from sale of guddes	162 19 6
(including sums received from John Smyth	
and Richard Haye & other items not listed above)	122 17 6
Thomas Thacker also received part of the	
total goods sold	

1 Letters and Papers. Foreign and Domestic, Henry VIII, Vol 7, British Library.
2 Ibid. Vol. 9, item 622, dated October 1535. Ap Rice was a former colleague of Legh.
3 Letters and Papers Henry VIII, Vol. 10 (1536), HMSO, 1887.
4 Letters and Papers of Henry VIII. Vol. 13/ii (1538), g.457/4, p. 177.
5 Joan d'Arcy, m.s.
6 British Library Add. Mss., 6698 folio 273-8 & 6714 folio 116-9 verso.

CHAPTER 5

RELIGIOUS LIFE AFTER THE REFORMATION

VALUABLES AND POSSESSIONS IN GRESLEY CHURCH, 1553 (EDWARD VI)

Cox details the report[1] by the Church Goods Commissioners on the contents of the church ten years after the sale to Henry Criche of the Priory lands:

'Gresley. Oct 5. John Kente curate. j chalice of silver gylte – iiij bells whereof Henry Creeche gent. Claimeth ij in the right of Greisley abbey (priory) – ij vestments the j of crymesyn damaske braunched the other of redd fustyen in apples – ij albes – j cope of grene and yelowe creaule – j crosse of brasse – ij aulter clothes – j corporas case of bleu chatalett – iiij towells – j hand-bell – j surples – j holywater canne of brasse – j pixe of brasse – j crosse clothe of silke off dyvers colers – j sacrying bell – j payre of sensors of brasse which be gone.'

Henry Criche had helped himself to two of the valuable bells, though as the history research group commented, it was not clear whether these were small altar bells or the large bells in the tower.[2] The brass censers were also missing.

The church had largely avoided the destruction of the rest of the dual-purpose building because the parishioners still needed a place for worship but an enormous shock had been administered to both church and community. Alongside the sweeping away of religious houses a revolution had also been occurring to the content of church services. The impact of this affected parishes at varying times: the first priest of post-dissolution Gresley, curate John Kent, was a Catholic, who still followed the old ritual, his period of office lasting

Scropton Church, drawn very shortly before complete rebuilding in 1856.
Note its near derelict state

The tithe barn at Swarkestone

Stapenhill village and stocks, 1824. Watercolour by P. Harrington

from about 1553 until 1557.[3]

The first Anglican vicar in Gresley was William Smythe (1576-79). His tenure, like John Kent's, was brief, in this period of consolidation interrupted by plots against the Queen, threats of invasion and repression of papists. The Authorised Version of the bible was not introduced in Gresley until Edward Bagshaw's curacy (1608-20).

The last Gresley Prior, John Oakley, had left with a pension of £6 per annum and two of the canons each with £5 16s 8d. The other canons were presumably given nothing on which to survive. The Gresley curate's stipend (£9 2s 0d in 1602)[4] was made up from the income of the church's glebe-lands, which also provided for the maintenance of the church's chancel – tithe payments from the parishioners sustaining the upkeep of the nave and the rest of the church.

In the manor of Aston-on-Trent, tithe payments from 240

acres provided income for the church, and there were 450 acres of glebeland.[5] A lord of the manor usually had the final say in his parish: Robert de Ferrers had once seen to it that two-thirds of Aston's tithes went to his favourite recipient, the Priory of Tutbury in the next county. When Gresley's tithes were abolished in 1849, they were being received from 350 acres of arable land and 730 acres of meadow.[6]

That the Elizabethan establishment feared organised dissent, particularly from the better educated, was shown by the cruel treatment of 'known papist' preachers. Three such alleged enemies of the state were put in goal in Derby, accused of preaching the Catholic faith. One Nicholas Garlick, who had been seven years a schoolmaster was, along with Richard Simpson and Robert Ludlam, sentenced to be hung, drawn and quartered – and this was carried out on 25 July 1582.[7]

A colleague of the three Catholic victims, John Fitzherbert, a victim of the anti-papist frenzy operating in Derbyshire at that time, was held in Derby gaol and then sent to the Fleet prison in London, where he died of gaol fever. Two of his daughters, both unmarried, were apprehended – and, as not infrequently happened with Catholics' children, taken from their parents. They were, it was explained later, 'placed in the custody of staunch conformists', with the hope that they might be persuaded to change their faith.[8]

The girls were put in the care of two parish priests, the brothers William and Richard Sale of Aston-on-Trent and Weston-on-Trent, men who were 'staunch adherents to the Elizabethan policy'.[9] In charge of the operation for their custody was chief papist-hunter the Earl of Shrewsbury, who wrote to the Privy Council:

"After or right hartie commendacions to your good Lo. We understand by your Lo. Its of the xixth of Julie last past that the two daughters of John Fitzharbert, Knight, committed by

yo L. direcions to the custody & gouverment of such persons as yo. L. thought most fitt about a yere past, having continued ever since in there obstinacie cannot be reduced into conformitie from their superstitious and erroneous opinions: forasmuch as they have been chargeable to the personnes to whom they were comitted, we think it fytt that some parte of the goods remayninge in yor Lo. Handes, appteyning to the said Fytzherberts may be sould at the best rate & value & satisfaction made thereof to the parties of such sumes of money as shalbe by defraying of their charges: And such afterwards to place them with some of their allies and kinsfolkes thereabouts, such as yor Lo shall judge to bee best affected, and wyllinge to travell for their conformitie. And so we wish our good Lo. Right hartilie well to fare. From the court at Otelandes the 21 of August 1589."
Yr Lo very assuring loving friends.

Under the patriotic Henry VIII, who had always professed himself 'a good Catholic', profoundly reformist steps had been taken by men who sought to promote, with state help, the essentials of a new religion. Bishop Latimer, in Worcester, commanded his priests to follow the royal will, that Latin be superseded in church services by English. But more revolutionary, under Henry's successor Edward, was Archbishop Cranmer's decision to introduce a Book of Common Prayer containing a mixed Lutheran-Calvinist confession.

These were times in which courtiers and placemen might survive whilst honest men and women of either faith suffered. Under 'Bloody' Mary, daughter of Henry and wife of Philip of Spain, Protestants were sought out and dispersed and their leaders cut down. A full Catholic mass returned, whilst Cranmer, Latimer and Ridley, leaders of the Protestant order, were burnt at the stake in Oxford in 1556.

Members of great and humble families could be equally at risk. In 1557 Joyce, daughter of Thomas Curzon of Croxall,

Tutbury Castle from an old engraving

having been arraigned for heresy, was burned at the stake in Coventry, seat of the diocese in which she had been born.[10] Elizabeth, whispered by Catholic militants to be the illegitimate daughter of Anne Boleyn, came to the throne in 1558, accompanied by unrest in the north, where there remained a large Catholic minority.

There existed a physical threat to the Crown from Elizabeth's cousin Mary Queen of Scots. Mary, forced by Protestants to vacate the Scottish throne, then made the fatal error of coveting that occupied by Elizabeth. Moving to England, Mary was seized, eventually arriving at the Tower of London and the place of execution. On her journey there, she was escorted from Derby to Tutbury by Thomas Gresley (knighted in 1603) in accordance with Gresley's position as Sheriff of Staffordshire (and by reason of his extensive properties in Derbyshire, Sheriff there as well).

Mary met her death in 1587, the year in which a posthumous attainder of high treason – one year after his death – was levelled against Sir Christopher Alleyn of Gresley and the Mote in north Kent on suspicion of having conspired with other Catholics (the Babington Plot) against Queen

THE CHURCH IN SOUTH DERBYSHIRE: 1602-3[16]

Parish	Incumbent	Status	Qualification (degree)	Preachers licence	Stipend £ s
Repton	Thomas Blander	Curate	Bach. of Artes	No preacher	x li
Misham	Thomas Asking	Curate	Master of Artes	A preacher by licence of Yorke	x li
Gresley	George Ward	Curate	No degree	No preacher	ix li
Hartshorne	William Dethicke	Parson	Bach. of Artes	No preacher	iij li ij In the Kinges books jd
Walton-upon-Trent	Edmund Clayton	Parson	No degree	No preacher	xvi li xviij In the Kinge's bookes
Melborne	William Kent	Curate	No degree	No preacher	vij li x tithes of the moiety
Eginton	Symon Prest	parson of one moeity of the living	Master of Artes	A public preacher by licence of the Bishop of Gloucester and Lichfield and Coventry	value of the moeity

Elizabeth. Alleyn had become owner of the estates of the former Gresley Priory, which lands had been sold first to Henry Criche who in turn had sold to John Seymour – and he to Alleyn.

Within a year of Elizabeth's accession there were enacted a fresh Oath of Supremacy (the first having been under her father) and Acts of Uniformity that restored the pre-Marian Liturgy. There was, on 28 April 1559, a further revision to the Book of Common Prayer, accompanied by a requirement that religious incumbents should sign their undertaking to use the Revised Book, failure to do which would lead to the forfeiture of their living. The response was less than whole-hearted, by one account only a third of Derbyshire's clergy being numbered among these assenters. They included the vicars of Walton-on-Trent and Ravenstone (the latter still in Derbyshire) but the vicar of Melbourne was said to have resigned his benefice before he could be asked to do so.[11]

In Derbyshire's High Peak most titled families were Catholic. Perhaps there was safety in numbers and it was more isolated. Further south, Sir Thomas Gerard of Etwall was summoned to London to answer a charge of recusancy. Belief, if bruited abroad, could be dangerous. Gerard at first escaped any penalty but was then taken to spend two substantial periods in the Tower – from 1567-1570 and again from September 1586 to August 1588, appearing in a 'list of false Papists as carry the countenances of gentlewomen and gentlemen' that had been drawn up by a Privy Council spy.[12]

Restiveness in the north, developing into open rebellion, produced calls for severe punishment of any identifiable rebel group. Thus Henry, Earl of Huntingdon, writing from York on 28 December 1572 to William Cecil, Lord Burghley; quoting from Articles issued by the Queen's Council of the North, stating commands that went out to county sheriffs: the opening order was pointed at the Catholic gentry who were held to be behind the rising.

"You are first to enquire and certify to us the names and addresses of all the known suspected papists, within your rule, the enemies of God and of good order, especially of such as do not come to church".

Signed by W. Burghley. Francis Walsingham, and four others of the Privy Council.[13]

Queen Elizabeth had been excommunicated by Pope Pius V, England had narrowly escaped invasion by the Armada in 1588 and, in the summer of 1596 an order was given to all sheriffs that where recusants had horses or armour, these were to be seized as constituting a potential threat to the realm.[14]

Indomitable men on either side of the religious war went to their deaths cheerfully, but there were ways of circumventing the law that all must attend the Established Church. Since 1581, wealthy Catholic gentlemen in Derbyshire had been able to compound for their absence from Church services by payment of £20 per month – a very considerable sum. Of this fine, one third "was enjoyed by the Queen, one third was given to the poor and one third was the perquisite of the informer."[15]

The vehemence of Elizabeth's orders for all to attend divine service suggested that authority was fearful of free-thinkers, but all preachers were encouraged to apply for licences, with the evident assumption that such men would be at the same time safe and acceptable to their congregations. In South Derbyshire, in 1602, there were only two preachers with licences, at Egginton and Measham. It has been suggested that, whilst officially the power of granting licences was vested in the Archbishop, it belonged in practice to the Queen and her Council. The bishops, as at Lichfield, according to this version, were 'ordered to issue and revoke licences according to political caprice'.[17]

Four of South Derbyshire's incumbents had degrees. A

Gresley Old Hall, built 1556-7 by Sir Christopher Alleyn, deriving much of its material from the ruined Gresley Priory. The Hall was afterwards sold to the Meynells and afterwards to the Gresleys.

Burton Observer

solitary Doctor of Divinity at Wirksworth was the county's only such dignitary but the appearance in the pulpit of their licensed preacher led to all but four of the Wirksworth congregation leaving 'in a clamourous fashion'.[18]

The pressure by conformists, albeit in a drastically altered Church begun by Henry VIII, was reflected in the Hundred of Repton and Gresley's nil-return of papists for 1634.[19]

It has been seen that the temperature of official concern rose sharply at times of external or domestic threat. In 1625 memories of Spanish Wars, plots and stratagems were still fresh in the mind. The Alleyns of Gresley were well-known for their Catholic affiliations, and Sir Francis Coke, writing to his brother Sir John, a member of the Privy Council, described a scene not untypical of middle-class households of that place and in that time. Despite failure to be registered, Catholics were still abroad. Sir Francis described what was found within 'one little house' in Castle Gresley, containing those who were undeniably and proudly Catholic – despite their not appearing on the Papist return.

'ROMISH RECUSANTS' (1625)[20]
1625, November 17, Trusley.
Sir Francis Coke to Sir John Coke, knight, one of
his Majesty's most honourable Privy Council.

A remembrance of such things as were observed in the house of Romish recusants and others suspected within the Hundreds of Morleston and Litchurch, Appletree, and Repton and Gresley in the county of Derby, at such times as the houses were searched by the Deputy Lieutenants of the said county for their arms and warlike weapons by commandment from the Lords of his Majesty's most honourable Privy Council in Novr. 1625.

At Castle Gresley, within the hundred of Repton and Gresley, there was in one little house (not above two bays and low built) six gentlewomen of very good fashion outwardly and well apparelled, one of them being an ancient gentlewoman called Mrs Tamworthy, with whom the rest sojourned; another of them was Captain Allen's wife, which Captain Allen had served the last year under the Archduchess, and was at London as she said; none of the said gentlewomen's husbands was there, save only one whose name I remember not. They were all recusants, and they had so many men and women servants that I marvel how they could lodge in so little a house. Every one of these gentlewomen had a riband of green and another of white silk tied in a kind of knot upon their left arm, and (as is reported) did use to give such ribands to divers of their friends and well wishers. I think these women were able to make more proselytes than twenty priests, for it is pestilent kind of cunning at Brisselcote (not far from Castle Gresley and in that hundred) being in the house of John Merry, gentleman, and half a mile remote from any town we found a Dutchman, by trade a painter, who was then drawing of the picture of one of these gentlewomen (which we had seen at Castle Gresley), beholding a crucifix painted before her a little higher that she might look up to it.

An English Church, owing allegiance first to the Crown, still felt it necessary to re-emphasise the break from Rome and guard against the Catholic remnant. There were political dangers from a restive parliament ready to challenge a king's divine right to rule and there were reasons to be wary of determined prophets who believed they were empowered to redefine a Christian's role. The severing of the link with Rome had given the nod to expansion of old sects: Baptists, offering redemption for all; Anabaptists and Calvinists with their severe doctrine offering alternatives of salvation and perdition. The revolt against the religious and royal authority also encouraged the appearance of new Christian rebels with a cause.

George Fox, Quaker

George Fox was born the son of a weaver in 1624, in Fenny Drayton, Leicestershire. King James I had entered a political crisis, with Puritans determined to resist any recovery of status by Catholics. Fox, a man of rare quality and complete integrity, dismissed what he saw as the trappings of religion and offered an alternative way for individual believers to communicate directly with God, dispensing with priests, churches, ritual, interpreters and all 'professors' (those who would make their living out of preaching). Under Charles I, Archbishop Laud, enemy of the Puritans and inclined to Catholic ritual, was executed in 1643. In 1649 Charles I was beheaded for holding himself higher than parliament and in the same year Fox was imprisoned at Nottingham. He had been convicted of disturbing a service. In his own account Fox had 'espied the great steeple-house' and was moved by the Lord 'to go out against yonder idol and against the worshippers therein.'[21]

In 1650 Fox was charged in Derby with blasphemy: he had been compelled, he said, to attend a lecture in church, after which he got into an altercation and 'there came an officer and took me by the hand, and said I must go before the magistrates.'[22]

> To the Master of the House of Correction in Derby, greeting.
>
> We have sent you herewithal the bodies of George Fox, late of Mansfield, in the county of Nottingham, and John Fretwell, late of Stainsby, in the county of Derby, husbandman, brought before us this present day and charged with the avowed uttering and broaching of divers blasphemous opinions contrary to a late Act of Parliament, which, upon their examination before us, they have confessed. These are therefore to require you forthwith, upon sight thereof, to receive them, the said George Fox and John Fretwell, into your custody, and therein safely to keep during the space of six months, without bail or mainprize, or until they shall find sufficient security to be of good behaviour, or be thence delivered by order from ourselves. Hereof you are not to fail. Given under our hands and seals this 30th day of October 1650. Ger. Bennett; Nath. Barton.[23]

Quakers did not have services, but meetings which could be in the house of a friend, and they came to refer collectively to their movement as one of Friends. In 1662 in a house at Swannington they were apprehended by an officer with a company of soldiers.

> 'There were some Friends out of Derbyshire, one of whom was named Thomas Fauks. And this Lord Beaumont (the officer) after he had asked all their names, bid his men set down that man's name Thomas Fox. But the Friend said his

George Fox and the rest were then gaoled in Leicester – his sixth period of imprisonment. This was the period of the Restoration and of vengeance against Puritans. The king's men were not well disposed towards the Quakers, of whom, by their tally, 1300 were in prison in 1662. By the Conventicle Acts of 1664 and 1667, meetings for worship were forbidden other than those held according to the practice of the Church of England. Where the meeting was held in a house, it was to consist of not more than four persons over 16 years of age beyond members of the same household.[25]

The Declaration of Indulgence in 1672 for a time showed a kinder face to minority faiths, withdrawing many existing sanctions, but there followed the Test Act of 1673, prohibiting Dissenters from holding public meetings.

In these troubled times, minds could be opened to men of inspiration. The Quakers carried dangers for government in their pacifist message that all violence was wrong, and there was a second count: Fox's repeated opposition to the imprisonment of 'tithe debtors' carried a direct challenge to both royalty and the Established Church.

A return by the Diocese of Lichfield and Coventry in 1677[26] showed Catholicism still strong in the north of Derbyshire, with 140 Catholics in Hathersage and 65 in Bakewell, contrasting with just fourteen in South Derbyshire outside Derby and four in the burgh of Derby itself.

101 Dissenters were registered for Derby and 103 for the rest of South Derbyshire: twenty came from Mickleover, sixteen each from Marston-on-Dove and Melbourne and nine from Etwall.

The spate of licences issued between 1763 and 1796 included a group in the area Smisby-Hartshorne-Ticknall-Melbourne. The whole licence concentration from 1689 onwards had been in the area south of the Trent, included Caldwell and Rosliston, and another pair of centres at

Packington and Ravenstone.

Normally an occupied house or just one room in it would be used for worship, but at Alvaston, in 1718 a 'newly-erected building' was given a licence and at Derby, in 1800, the Quakers were licensed to use a room in a former silk mill, situated in a court off Irongate, belonging to John Cox.[27] In 1802, the Baptists were allowed to use a new house in Bucknall's Yard, Ticknall.

There could well have been one law for Dissenters and another for Catholics who, when George I came to the throne in 1714 were still subject to many penalties and injunctions – needing a licence to travel more than five miles from their homes and being debarred from sitting in parliament. One of the recurrent periods of danger, particularly for the Catholic minority, came in 1715 with the Scots' invasion of North-West England in 1715. Old laws, re-activated, forbade the keeping of arms in Catholic homes and a new law was passed, doubling the land-tax on Roman Catholic holdings.[28] George I had signed the necessary orders in 1716, but certain named Derbyshire Catholics – six from South Derbyshire – as a reward for their having stood aside from the Jacobite rebels, were given exemption from the confiscation of property that had been inflicted on others.

PROTECTION FOR NAMED RECUSANTS, 6 APRIL 1716[29]

Name	Status	Residence	Property value		
			£	s	d
John Alleyne	Gent*	Weston	89	17	0
Robert Freeman	Gent.	Weston	3	16	0
Anne Savage	Widow	Weston	20	0	0
Mary Simpson		Barton Blount	344	17	6
George Pigg	Gent.	Osmaston	(omitted)		
Robert Beaumont	Esq.	Barrow-upon-Trent	86	4	0

There is a second sum given for John Alleyne, of £91 1s 4d

Parish	Sex	Age	Occupation	Resident
Barrow	M	36	gentleman	36 years
	M	33	apothecary	33
	M	31	gentleman	31
	W	37		37
Barton Blount	W	60		50
Church Broughton	W	40	servant	7
Derby	M	40	reputed priest	
St. Peters	M	50	blacksmith, his wife (and 5 children)	
	W	70	pauper	
	W	38		
	M	35	joiner	
St. Werburghs	W	60		9
All Saints	M	36	clock maker	
		30	his wife 2 sons and 4 daughters	
		22	his brother	
Repton	M	75	farmer (6 sons Protestants)	50
Sutton on the Hill	M	54	farmer	21
Weston upon Trent	M	60	farmer his wife, 4 sons, 2 daughters	60 60
	M	65	farmer	65
	M	70	do.	70
	W	57		57
			2 sons, 1 daughter servants.	
	M	62	labourer	62

18TH CENTURY CHURCH FINANCES: TITHES AND DUES

On the more fertile land towards the Trent and away from the Coal Measures of Swadlincote and Gresley, Abraham Swaine, Vicar of Stapenhill, made an inventory in 1719, via his bishop's officers, of the dues owed to his church by the inhabitants of Stapenhill, as well as those of Stanton, Newhall and Caldwell.

The reckoning was set out in the terrier of the "Glebe Lands and other profits whatsoever belonging to the Vicar of Stapenhill in the Diocese of Lichfield and Coventry and in the county and archdeaconry of Derby, taken February 2nd 1705 by me Abr. Swaine Vicar."[31]

The people of Stapenhill farmed four huge fields named, in descending order of size, Lenway, Water, Ridgeway and Wood fields, amounting in total to about 40 acres. From all the tenants tithes were due, with just one exception – the plot attached to John Warren's tenement or cottage, which had from "time immemorial Custom been excused from serving the offices of Constable, Churchwarden and Overseer of the Poor and from paying any Levies to the Church."

Only corn was excepted from the variety of farm produce that furnished the tithes: there remained pigs, geese, wool, lambs, calves, colts, eggs, hay, hemp, flax and "all manner of

Gresley Parish Church (1789), reproduced from a drawing by the Rev. R.Randall Rawlins. To the left is the arch of the Austin Canons priory – all that remained in the 18th century from the destruction wrought by Henry VIII's dissolution.

(in Derby Local Studies Library, reproduced by kind permission of Derby City Libraries).

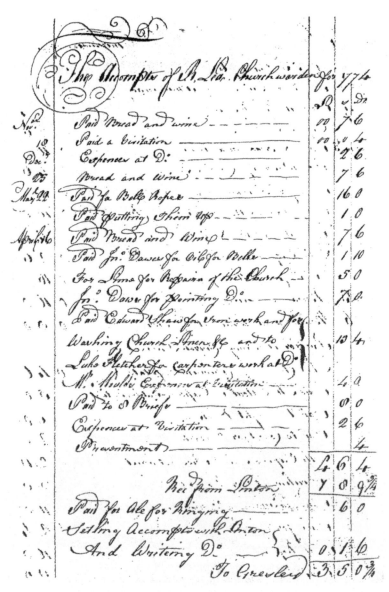

A Churchwarden's accounts

Derbyshire County Council: Derbyshire Record Office, D3335/1/1.

Reproduced by permission of the County & Diocesan Archivist.

68

Fruit and Easter Offerings" that were paid to the Vicar in kind.

Inhabitants of Stanton and Newhall, on the other hand, for a very long time had been allowed to commute their tithe debt into a cash payment: for the townships, "£6 3s per year – three pounds on Lady day and the other three pounds at Michaelmas."[32]

By a similar arrangement with the inhabitants of Caldwell dated September 1676 they paid the vicar of Stapenhill tithes of six pounds yearly on St. John the Baptist's day.

METHODISTS AND OTHER NONCONFORMISTS

Methodism, like industry, arrived relatively late on the South Derbyshire coalfield. Further north, the Presbyterians Edward Fleminge and John Carter had been licensed in 1689 to preach in their houses in Findern. During the last decade of the 18th century Wesleyans from the Gresley area had met in a cottage in Jack's i' th' Hole until the money was found

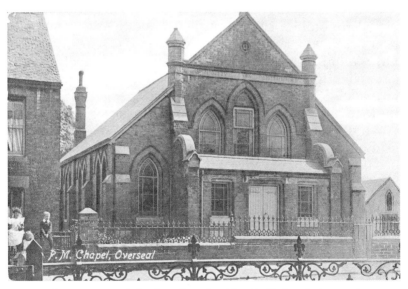

The Primitive Methodist Chapel in Woodville Road, Overseal.

The Primitive Methodist Chapel and Schools in Market Street, Church Gresley

in 1806 to build a chapel on the edge of Gresley Common later occupied by the pottery of Messrs. T.G. Green and Co. Ltd. Within a short distance from the new chapel was the Granville Colliery, and although the original building was taken down in 1816, similar (Wesleyan) chapels were put up: in 1816 at Swadlincote and (the 'Ebenezer' chapel) at Woodville in 1817. Methodists in Gresley – Wesleyans leading the way, Primitive Methodists following – had a positive educational role through the provision of Sunday Schools.

RELIGION AND RECREATION

The first Methodist chapels to be sanctioned – if not at first explicitly – in South Derbyshire had multiple functions of teaching and cultural expression. There were many who learned to read through accompanying parents to chapel and thence to Sunday school. Through these institutions,

Er.Hall, ED.Hall, T.Booth, J.Arnold, H.O.Thirsk, E.Bacon, E.Mansfield

G.T.Knighton, A.Evans, J.Leech, A.H.Sharpe, P.R.Tunnicliffe, D.Sibley, F.W.Robinson, G.Jones, G.Hull, F.R.Walton

A.Walton, W.Jackson, F.T.Moore, W.Kilbourne, A.H.Robinson, G.Fairbrother, W.Foskett, R.Trussell, S.Evans, W.Turner, A.Jones, B.Powell

E.E.Baxter, R.Tunnicliffe, J.W.Smith, J.Starkey, G.Walton, J.T.Lea, J.T.Walton, T.Vallance, H.L.Evans, J.W.Wilton
(Secretary) (Conductor) (Treasurer)

L.Daws, G.A.Mansfield, J.Walton, J.J.Horsfield, J.T.Langley, T.L.Clark

CHURCH GRESLEY P.M. MALE VOICE CHOIR, 1910

By courtesy of Roy Atkins

71

CHURCH GRESLEY P.M. MALE VOICE CHOIR, 1923

J.Leech, F.Smedley, R.Goacher, J.Warren, A.Orme, W.Jones, W.Parker, J.Winfield
J.Clamp, W.Warren, A.Halsey, E.Bacon, W.Lowe, J.B.Fowkes, H.Perry, W.Langley, C.Wilkins, C.Ball, E.Mansfield, L.Winfield, F.Calow
W.Woollett, C.R.Ford, J.Harrison, J.W.Boam, T.Boam, A.Wood, F.J.Brown, J.Kirk, C.Watson, W.Peace, R.G.Watson, F.Eames, W.Sutton
E.R.Cross, C.Hart, R.Burbank, F.Morgan, G.Hull, T.L.Clark, J.Starkey, G.Knighton, W.Jackson, S.Barker, H.Buck

By courtesy of Roy Atkins

72

later generations were introduced to music at a high level. There was much intermarriage between Wesleyan and Primitive Methodist families, with descendants of Moses Jones marrying into a (Walton) family also of great musical promise. It was the brothers George and John Thomas Walton who in 1904 founded the Male Voice Choir, based on the Primitive Methodist Church in Church Gresley. The Choir went on to achieve the ultimate honour of winning the semi-national Eisteddfod, in 1927 against competition from five other choirs, including two from Wales.[33]

One notable feature of local interest concerned the involvement of businessmen: notably Sir Herbert Wragg, the sanitary pipe manufacturer and Haldane Robinson, director of Benjamin Robinson Ltd., who were in turn Presidents of the Choir. From another industrialist came an infusion of money for the brother religious group with a decision by Edward Ensor who committed himself during the period 1866-1880 to provide the Wesleyans with a chapel. This, the Pool Works Chapel, was erected by a novel contrivance, Mr

The old York Road Methodist Chapel, Church Gresley,
replaced by a new church in 1971

Ensor having prevailed upon his workers, or at least a good number of them, to contribute to the cause of Methodism. They would work overtime for Mr Ensor, passing on the equivalent of their labour to the chapel. Unfortunately, when Mr Ensor experienced some financial problems of his own, and liquidation followed, the landowner foreclosed on the project and the chapel ceased for a time to operate. It was able to reopen in 1881, and eventually, Wesleyan and Primitive Methodist churches were demolished and replaced in 1971 by a single multi-purpose building.[35] The York Road Methodist Church had meanwhile celebrated its Golden Jubilee in 1948.

1 Cox, op. cit. Churches of Derbys., vol. III, p. 372.
2 Spavold, op. cit., p. 266.
3 Ibid.
4 Spavold, op. cit., p. 262.
5 Glover, op. cit., vol. II, p. 59.
6 Spavold, op. cit., p. 215.
7 VCH Derbys., op. cit. pp. 25-6.
8 Cox, op. cit. Three Centuries of Derbyshire Annals, Vol. I, p. 257.
9 Ibid.
10 Glover, op. cit., Vol. II, p. 334.
11 VCH Derbys. Vol. II, p. 20.
12 Ibid., p. 24.
13 Ibid.
14 Acts of the Privy Council, Vol. 26, p. 294.
15 Cox, op. cit. Three Centuries of Derbyshire Annals, Vol. I, p. 255.
16 Cox, op. cit. Churches of Derbys., Vol. I, pp. 246-7.
17 Cox, op. cit. Churches of Derbys., Vol. I, p. 245.
18 Ibid., p. 244.
19 VCH Derbys. Vol. II, p. 27.
20 Cox, op. cit. Three Centuries of Derbyshire Annals, Vol. I, p. 284.
21 Fryer, Jonathan, (ed.), George Fox and the children of the light, Kyle Cathie, c.1991, p. 26.
22 Ibid., p. 32.
23 Ibid., p. 33.
24 Ibid., p. 160.
25 Brayshaw, A. Neave, The Personality of George Fox, Allenson & Co: London, 1933, p. 137 (note).
26 VCH. Derbys., Vol. II., pp. 39-40.
27 Cox, op. cit. Three Centuries of Derbyshire Annals, p. 368.

28 Ibid.
29 Glover, op. cit. Appendix, p. 84.
30 Catholic Record Society, 1989, House of Lords Library.
31 Brit. Lib. Add. Mss. 1674. f. 287, quoting the report of the Rev. Swaine.
32 Ibid.
33 Hall, M., 'Gresley Male Voice Choir 1904-1984'.
34 Early history of Methodism in Gresley, (M. Hall, Wesleyan Church archive).Smith, J. & R., Parish Church of Gresley, St.George and St. Mary – a brief history and guide (undated), p. 16.

CHAPTER 6

POVERTY AND RELIEF

Poverty, in a feudal society, reflected the gap between the small number of rich and very large number of disadvantaged. The majority of the people had no possibility of escaping from the station into which they had been born. The king owned much of the best land, and in the royal forest a man who poached game to alleviate his family's hunger could be hanged for the offence. Most of the people were trapped only slightly above subsistence level, where plague, pestilence or a succession of bad harvests could produce economic disaster.

Relief from the severest crises in family life could come from alms distributed by the parish priest or his assistant, the churchwarden. Where there was a religious house such as a priory, the poor could go along to the gate on festivals, holy or other times designated for the receipt of broken meats left over from the monks' repast or purposely put aside for relief. More substantial help came from pence left by bequest to the poor. An important role of a house could be to service link roads in their area: the abbeys of Burton and Merevale saw to the basic maintenance of the key road through Castle Gresley and Acresford that connected their two houses. Bridges were maintained and mended and watercourses cleared – supplying useful employment for unskilled labour. But damage could be done to amenities: according to Glover, in the reign of Edward I, the bishop of Chester and the abbot of Dale had 'injured the stream of the Derwent by their dams or wears.'[1]

There was however a cost to the people's dependence on the church. Even those with only a small property would have an obligation through the payment of tithes to maintain their priest's stipend.

The Reformation, through the introduction of a Prayer Book in English, made it more intelligible to the literate minority, but in important ways the reformed church was often more distant and its officers less available, an important consideration during the latter part of the Tudor period, when there was significant growth in trade, internal and external. New social demands were made upon authority, with a sudden increase in the number of aimless, shiftless poor people.

Tudor monarchs had a new legal arm to deal with economic crisis after Henry VIII introduced the office of Justice of the Peace. Under Vagrancy Acts, this representative of the Crown was required to distinguish between 'impotent' (vulnerable) and able-bodied poor. Anyone without roots and charged with imposing his presence upon a community could, on a J.P.'s command, be whipped out of a town. For generations, the destitute had had recourse only to the parish priest or his churchwarden; there could be a dole of charity pence, or of fuel from the South Derbyshire coalfield. A major change came with the Poor Law Acts of 1597 and 1601, introducing the statutory office of Overseer of the Poor and defining his duties. The overseer would need to be a man of some substance, probably a yeoman, elected by the parish. Two such overseers would be chosen by the property-owners of a parish, having access to the product of a poor rate. Overseers would need to be able to read and write and draw up simple accounts. In 1597, John Wakefield was elected overseer for Church Gresley.[2]

There was a special role for the new officer in administering charitable bequests to needy individuals that parish priests in the past would have found it difficult to handle. A legacy was made to 'two poor women' of Stapenhill remembered in the will of Edward Robinson of Gresley in 1602.[3] An attractive element of charitable bequests from now on was to use the trust principle. William Ward, leaving a bequest to the poor of Gresley parish in 1634, appointed a group of trustees to look after the money.[4]

After the Poor Law Acts of 1597 and 1601, provision was made for overseers and churchwardens to build cottages for poor persons on waste land. A petition for such houses to be built in Derby was presented in 1639, although one commentator reported[5] that little attention was paid to the quality of materials used.

A happier development was the contemporary provision of almshouses. The group of twelve such houses built by the Countess of Shrewsbury in Derby in 1597-99, with accommodation for eight men and four women, all of them to be paid the very acceptable sum of 2s 6d per week, as well as 'two gowns per year'.[6] Glover gives details of the similar almshouses bequeathed in the will to his son by Robert Wilmot of Chaddesden in 1638, the occupants also to be given two gowns yearly and, every two years, the men would receive a 'red cap of about 2s a piece' and at Christmas 'thirty yards of linen cloth at 12d the yard', to be distributed among the ten poor people – gifts which were not insignificant for that day. Almshouses were also established at Etwall by Sir John Port in 1556, rebuilt in 1681, and at Netherseal where Richard Johnson provided almshouses for nine poor people with an endowment of

£182 yearly.

A weekly dole of 2s 6d in relief was given to able-bodied poor required to work on breaking stones. The product of a mixed-ability labour force, poorly supervised, was predictably inadequate to improve the road system. More positive were the moves taken in Derbyshire under the early Stuarts to intervene when the price of basic foods rose out of reach of many people. In February 1631, measures were taken to make available to the market large supplies of grain, to be sold direct to the public and not to dealers.[7]

The 18th century saw major changes in both town and village as farm strips were enclosed into coherent holdings and cottage industry had either to work with or to be threatened by factory products. In 1759, Derbyshire's Jedediah Strutt, with his invention of a rib machine[8] for stocking manufacture, had taken the first step to changing work patterns in the Middle Derwent valley and later in Derby itself. Earnings in the hosiery industry declined outside Strutt's own operation, and there were inevitable casualties among the small men working from home and relying on the participation of their wives and children. There was no cushion to unemployment other than the overseer's dole.

Whilst earnings in hosiery in Derby in 1777 could be as little as 10s per week, this was better than the farm labourer's wage level, which had fallen before 1800 to less than 8s per week. Small farmers whose property was not freehold could find themselves, after enclosure, with no house and no garden plot, no poultry, pigs or cattle. If the labourer or ex-farmer had gone poaching with a gun in 1800 he would have been liable on conviction to fourteen years' transportation.[9]

RELIEF AND ANALYSIS

Revenue and expenditure for Derbyshire were tabulated[10] under hundreds, with the Hundred of Repton and Gresley

The Accoumpts of George Buckley Overseer of the
Poor of Church Gresley from March 1830

		£	s	d
March 30	My Journey to Swarkestone		6	
31	My Journey to Repton		5	
	Paid for Appointments		13	
April 3	Paid W^m. Ordidge 4 weeks at 2		8	
	Paid W^m. Marshall & child 4 weeks at 4		16	
	Paid W^m. Mason 4 weeks at 2		8	
	Paid W^m. Smith 4 weeks at 1-6		6	
	Paid W^m. Woodward 4 weeks at 1		4	
	Paid Willm. Bird 4 weeks at 1		4	
7	Paid for one Dozⁿ. of sparrows			3
8	Paid for New Book		2	
May 1	Paid W^m. Ordidge 5 weeks at 2		10	
	Paid W^m. Marshall & child 5 weeks at 4	1		
	Paid W^m. Mason 5 weeks at 2		10	
	Paid W^m. Smith 5 weeks at 1..6		7	6
	Paid W^m. Woodward 5 weeks at 1		5	
	Paid Willm. Bird 5 weeks at 1		5	
7	Paid for 2 hedgehogs at 2 each			4
	Paid for a Letter			2
22	Paid for 3 Dozⁿ. and half of sparrows at 3			10
29	Paid for sighning poor rate		2	
	Paid Joseph Woodward when Ill		4	4
June 5	Paid W^m. Ordidge 4 weeks at 2		8	
	Paid W^m. Marshall & child 4 weeks at 4		16	
	Paid W^m. Mason 4 weeks at 2		8	
	Paid W^m. Smith 4 weeks at 1..6		6	
	Paid W^m. Woodward 4 weeks at 1		4	
	Paid Willm. Bird 4 weeks at 1		4	

The Accounts of George Buckley
Routine disbursements under the Old Poor Law
Derbyshire County Council: Derbyshire Records Office, D2112 A/PO 1/2
Reproduced by permission of the County and Diocesan Archivist

80

having charged their ratepayers four shillings in the pound of their rateable value in 1803 towards the relief of the poor.[11] The county expected some income back from its houses of industry, but of the total of such receipts for Derbyshire as a whole, the biggest sum (£70 out of a little more than £200) came from the city of Derby and under £10 from the Repton and Gresley Hundred.[12] The Shardlow Council had been one of the first regionally to offer direct help over rents for pauper cottages at the turn of the century, with as little as 3d and not more than 1s a week having been asked of tenants in 1803.[13]

The ranks of the poor had grown during the Napoleonic wars and there had been hard winters in 1794-95 and 1789-99.[14] Poor rate expenditure per head in Derbyshire increased by a half between 1803 and 1813, with part of the blame by a contemporary observer[15] attributable to demobilisation from the wars, decrease in demand for agricultural labour due to greater efficiency on farms and, industrially, the destructive competition from large enterprises in Derby and Nottingham. There was lack of expression of popular despair in an unrepresentative parliament, and some violence in the valleys north of Derby, which the authorities were fearful would become more general.

South Derbyshire was radically affected by the decision of the Speenhamland (Berkshire) magistrates who met on 6 May 1795.[16] They established as a subsistence norm the staple loaf of 8lbs 4ozs: this, they said, would 'rate Husbandry Wages'. If the loaf cost 1s, 'a poor and industrious Man' should have 'for his own support' 3s weekly, with the increase for a family man and to meet a dearer loaf,[17] and as the 3s could be part wage and part relief it tended to become the basic measure of subsistence and there were soon grounds for unease that unscrupulous employers would profit from the new system to pay shrunken wages in the knowledge that they would be made up.

The end of the 18th century saw rising unemployment and great distress even among those still working. Not all change was to the detriment of the poor: at Shardlow, between village and river ran the Grand Trunk Canal eventually connecting with the Trent, and in 1801 an agreement was signed between canal company and the Shardlow and Wilne Parish Council. At the general Quarter Sessions in Derby on 14 April, the company undertook to meet one third of the expenditure needed from rates to support the poor. The most serious negative aspect of the industrial change had been the displacement by business-men with capital of the jobs previously done by framework knitters working from home, Shardlow Parish records for 8 January 1812 include the item:

"Resolved that a frame be procured for Roberts and in the meantime that he shall go to House Row (the House of Industry) for 4s a week, the parish supplying the remainder of his support."[18]

Shardlow Council reacted to a deteriorating situation:

"Any Poor Person seeking redress whose place of abode is more than 6 miles from the residence of the Visitor has the option of applying to any Magistrate in the Neighbourhood or to the Visitor as may be most convenient or conducive to the ends of Justice."[19]

This resolution touched on what was viewed by parliament as the increasingly critical problem of controlling and limiting local liability for poor relief.

EARLY WORKHOUSES

From 1724, in the ninth year of George I's reign,[20] parishes were permitted to build workhouses with parish funds. In 1738, Dale Abbey combined with Ilkeston and neighbouring

Netherseal Almhouses founded by RIchard Johnson

Etwall Almshouses founded by Sir John Port

parishes to build a workhouse on Dale ('or Stanley') Moor.[21] Further south, under the Gilbert Act of 1782, the Rosliston Incorporation organised pauper accommodation in a joint workhouse for Rosliston itself and the parishes of Cauldwell, Coton-in-the-Elms and Linton.[22] In 1803 trustees of the inhabitants of Shardlow leased from Leonard Fosbrook 25 cottages which were let to the poor at rents of 3d to 1s a week. A Poor House or House of Industry for Shardlow was built. It cost £1,200 and opened in 1812, complete with Guardians of the Poor. From the start it served Shardlow – Wilne and their neighbours, to a total of 24 parishes.[23]

Shardlow's House of Industry gave a picture of a transient population. The institution's high proportion of children and large seasonal fluctuations in numbers reflected the precarious economic climate for a mainly agricultural community.

SHARDLOW HOUSE OF INDUSTRY, 1820[24]

Daily average accommodated

	Adults	Children
Jan	67	33
Feb	60	27
Mar	60	29
Apr	53	31
May	46	30
Jun	45	30
July	40	27
Aug	42	30
Sep	38	27
Oct	39	29
Nov	41	33
Dec	52	37

Shardlow Parish Council, having taken the courageous

	Men.	Women.	Boys under Ten years	Girls under Ten Years.	Total.
Admitted since the last account..........................	..	..	..	..	
Discharged ditto..					
Present numbers in the House............................	22	18	10	10	50
Desertions..	..	..	..	..	
Deaths...	..	..	..	..	
Sick List..	2	2	..	..	
Employed in manufacturing Hemp	..	..	..	..	
Ditto ditto, Grinding Corn	5	..	..	..	
Ditto ditto, Framework Stockings	1	1	..	..	
Ditto ditto, List Shoes	..	..	..	..	
Ditto ditto, Whip Cord.................................	..	..	..	..	
Ditto ditto, winding Cotton............................	..	..	..	..	
Ditto ditto, List Carpeting.............................	..	..	..	..	
Ditto ditto, the Kitchen, &c...........................	..	3	4	3	
Ditto ditto, running Lace..............................	3	4	4	3	
Ditto ditto, Seaming..................................	..	..	..	..	
Ditto ditto, Sewing...................................	..	7	6	7	
Old, infirm and unable to work............................	10	..	..	..	
Under punishment in the House of Industry..............	..	..	..	..	
Ditto in the Derby House of Correction...................	..	..	..	..	
Employed in Whitewashing &c	1	..	..	..	

Price of Provisions at the last Market; viz.—

At Derby, the 26 of Sept.   At Loughborough, the   of

Beef per lb. 5 ½ 7   Beef per lb.

Mutton, do. 5 ½ 7   Mutton do.

Pork, do.   Pork, do.

Bot. the Beef of Mr. Wm. Cookayne at 5 ½ p. lb.

JAMES STORER, PRINTER & BOOKBINDER, CORN MARKET, DERBY.

Employment in Shardlow House of Industry, 1834

TNA (PRO) MH12 2060

decision to finance permanent provision for paupers, had to have a care to address their legal liabilities – in particular the problem of eligibility. This was covered by a statute, 59 Geo. III (cap.12), that set down the residential terms for admittance to the workhouse or House of Industry.

Applicants with a settlement in Shardlow would automatically qualify. Otherwise the Visitor to the House of Industry would be called on to adjudicate, and as regards residential eligibility, the statute further stating that any Poor Person seeking redress whose place of abode was more than six miles from the residence of the Visitor had the option of applying to any magistrate in the neighbourhood "or to the Visitor as may be most Convenient or Conducive to the ends of Justice."[25]

1 Glover, op. cit., Vol. II, p. 376.
2 Spavold, op. cit., p. 272.
3 Ibid., p. 273.
4 Ibid., p. 272.
5 VCH Derbys. Vol. II, p. 179.
6 Glover, op. cit. Vol. II, p. 481.
7 VCH Derbys. II, p. 179.
8 VCH Derbys. II, p. 367.
9 Gregg, Pauline, A social and economic history of Britain 1760-1980, 1982, p. 32.
10 Farey, John, General view of the agriculture and minerals of Derbyshire, Vol II, 3 vols., London, 1811-17, verso, p. 31.
11 Ibid.
12 Ibid., item 9.
13 Collier, R.E., Notes on History of Shardlow, Collection of Jeff Clifton, p. 14.
14 Floud, Roderick & McCloskey, Donald N., (eds.), Economic History of Britain since 1700, 2 vols., Cambridge University Press, 1994, p. 81.
15 Eden, Sir Frederick Morton, The State of the Poor, Vol. 2, London, 1797, p. 29.
16 English Historical Documents, Vol. XI item 331, British Library.
17 Minutes of the Berkshire Justices 6 May 1795, British Library.
18 Collier, op. cit, p. 10.
19 Collier, op. cit., p. 12.
20 VCH Derbys. Vol. II, p. 1889.
21 Ibid.
22 PRO. MH 11233
23 Collier, op. cit. Notes, p. 10.
24 Collier, op. cit. Notes p. 13.
25 Collier, op. cit. Notes p. 12.

CHAPTER 7

A NEW POOR LAW

Poor Law Unions at the borders of Staffordshire, Derbyshire and Leicestershire, 1st January 1852

Note: W indicates location of Union Workhouses.
Source: Humphrey Southall and Institute of British Geographers,
survey of Poor Law Union Boundaries 1997

A new law became necessary when the Vagrancy Act of the early Tudors and the Poor Law Acts of Queen Elizabeth I became more and more unable to deal with the public burden of relief. Eventually Parliament demanded a national solution to the pressures on local resources and the resulting Poor Law Amendment Act of 1834 produced a network of unions formed out of groups drawn from existing parishes. Ratepayers of each parish would elect onto a union board guardians who would each need to own property valued at £40 per annum.

The Amendment Act was notable for its strict and stern disapproval of poverty, which was said by the Poor Law Commissioners to derive from "fraud, indolence or improvidence."[1] Every Union board was to have its own substantial workhouse, with out-relief confined to the genuinely helpless: the old, infirm or sick. New workhouses would house the able-bodied paupers, but would be designedly unwelcoming and spartan, offering conditions 'less eligible' than those of the lowest-paid independent labourer.

Originally it was intended that all able-bodied poor would be confined within the gates, but there was then an administrative change of mind. Employment could be provided outside the workhouse, but only on the principle "that all who receive work from the parish shall work for the parish exclusively, as hard as, and for less wages than, independent labourers work for individual employers."[2] Applicants from a parish seeking relief would need to produce evidence of having a settlement there. One element of the problems involved in workhouse accommodation for the aged sick or infirm was addressed by the Medical Officer for Burton:

"old people of sixty years of age and upwards may be allowed 1oz of tea, 5oz of butter and 7oz of sugar per Week in lieu of milk Porridge for Breakfast if deemed expedient to make this change. Children under nine years of age, to be dieted at discretion; above nine, the same quantities as Women. Sick to be dieted as directed by the Medical Officer to the Burton Union. September 1845."[3]

Burton Union Workhouse Dietary for Able – bodied men and women' 25 September 1845.

		Breakfast		Dinner							Supper		
		Bread	Milk Porridge	Cooked Meat	Cooked Potatoes	Day of Diet Stew	Suet Pudding	Irish Stew	Yeast Dumpling	Bread	Cheese	Milk Porridge	Broth
		oz	Pints	oz	oz	Pints	oz	Pints	oz	oz	oz	Pints	Pints
Sunday	Men	7	1½	5	1½							1½	
	Women	6	1½	4	1½							1½	
Monday	Men	7	1½			1½				7	1		
	Women	6	1½			1				6	1		
Tuesday	Men	7	1½				16			7		1½	
	Women	6	1½				14			6		1½	
Wednesday	Men	7	1½	5	1½					7			1½
	Women	6	1½	4	1½					6			1½
Thursday	Men	7	1½					2		7		1½	
	Women	6	1½					1½		6		1½	
Friday	Men	7	1½						12	7		1½	
	Women	6	1½						12	6		1½	
Saturday	Men	7	1½			1½				7	1		
	Women	6	1½			1				6	1		

Burton Union Workhouse

PRO. MH.12 - 11235

89

There followed an argument between Burton and Whitehall: when would bread or potatoes best accompany the twice-weekly leg-of-beef stew?

There could be a difference between an apparently appetising menu and what actually appeared at table: cooked meat with potatoes twice weekly for dinner, likewise leg of beef stew, but would the potatoes be edible? Plenty of milk porridge, but was all of Oliver Twist's gruel a piece of his author's imagination. After Dickens wrote conditions are said greatly to have improved – if not everywhere.

The problems resulting from an individual's crossing of a Union boundary were illustrated in the Shardlow area in 1839, when Mary Coxon confronted the Poor Law Commissioners over the stoppage of her relief. The unequal struggle was chronicled by Stephen Dumelow, Chief Clerk to the Shardlow Union.

(i) The Workhouse Test; Reasons for applicability: the applicant was unable to assist herself and her 3 children entirely without help. The Test (of thus qualifying for entry to a workhouse) 'was consequently fully proved' in Mr. Dumelow's words. (ii) Results of examination in July 1839: a) The applicant was a woman of very good character, without settlement in the Union; b) As a binder of shoes she could expect to earn 5s per week and could 'with a little more in aid maintain her family', until the children were old enough to start work. (iii) Shardlow Union Secretary's letter of 4 Nov. 1839 to Poor Law Commissioners. No such work could be obtained for M. C. 'in any Parish within the District, nor any House found for her'. Therefore the Union Board asks for 'this case to be relieved out of the Union'. (iv) Internal memo of the Poor Law Commissioners 6 Nov 1839. "The Commissioners will not object to taking one of Mary Coxon's children into the Workhouse but they object to allowing her relief while non-resident". (v) Commissioners' letter of 7 Nov. 1839 from Somerset House. 'The Commissioners will not object to the Guardians taking one of Mary Coxon's children in the Workhouse if the Guardians think it expedient to adopt this course under the circumstances of the case, but the Commissioners regret to find themselves precluded from meeting the wishes of the [Shardlow] Board of Guardians so far as to sanction relief to Mary Coxon whilst non-resident'.[4]

Given its financial constraints and the importance to the House of Industry, of income from work the Shardlow of 1834 had to be conscious of its numbers of aged, infirm and sick unable to contribute to production. Such an economic concern could hardly be profitable. Interestingly though, girls over ten were classed as women, becoming thus a significant pool of labour outside the workhouse.

The list of activities available at Shardlow was typical of a small settlement near to much larger concentrations – Derby, Loughborough, Nottingham – with important textile operators in wool, silk, hemp, lace and to a lesser extent, cotton. Workhouse populations reflected the misery of workers dispossessed by the technological change in textile production.

It was inevitable that a price would be exacted from the recipient of relief. Good order and discipline, with punishment for infringement, were essential features of the residential provisions that were meant to deter rather than welcome those who might be eligible for help.

The General Order (1841) on workhouse rules was so designed as to ensure that the inmate with exaggerated symptoms of 'feeling poorly' would be placed on the same level of lawlessness as one who threatened the safety of others. The malefactor who misbehaved twice within one week called on his head a magisterial set of consequences:

'It shall be lawful for the master of the workhouse, with or without the direction of the Board of Guardians, to punish any 'disorderly' person who had, for example, made 'any noise' when silence is ordered to be kept – the punishment to consist of substituting, during 'a time not greater than forty-eight hours, for his or her dinner, as prescribed by the dietary, a meal consisting of eight ounces of bread, or one pound of cooked potatoes, and also by withholding from him during the same period all butter, cheese, tea, sugar or broth, which such paupers would otherwise receive at any meal during the time aforesaid.'[5]

The Poor Law guardians, whose job it was to supervise the administration of the Burton workhouse and the welfare of its inmates, were drawn from the whole catchment area served by the workhouse. There was unsurprisingly a controlling interest by the business class of Burton, the Union's only large town, but an effort was made to draw also from the larger Derbyshire villages. As on other Midlands boards, there was a strong leaning towards the farming interest.

BURTON UNION, GUARDIANS OF THE POOR[6]

Gresley and South Derbyshire representatives, 10 April 1845

Elected guardian	Profession	Resident in
Thomas Burton	Farmer	Church Gresley
William Timms	do	Cadley Hill, Castle Gresley
The Rev. Theodore Echalaz	Clerk	The Vicarage, Lullington
Richard Foster	Farmer	Findern
Thomas Pratt	do	Cauldwell
William Smith	do	Drakelow
John Wain (sen.)	do	Bretby

The Derbyshire (Shardlow) Union choice of Guardians

Workhouse Form
Task of Work.

$\qquad$ *Shardlow* $\qquad$ UNION.

ORDERED :—By the Guardians of the *Shardlow* Union, at a Meeting of the Board, held this *sixth* day of *May* $\qquad$ One thousand eight hundred and forty-*four* ,—

THAT the Master of the Workhouse of the *Shardlow* *female* Union, do set every adult person not suffering under any temporary or permanent infirmity of body, being an occasional poor person who shall be relieved in the said Workhouse, in return for the food and lodging afforded to such person, to perform the following Task of Work, that is to say :—* *to pick one pound weight of Oakum in a proper and customary manner* $\qquad$

Here insert the kind and amount of work to be performed.

PROVIDED THAT no such person shall be detained against ~~his or~~ her will for the performance of such Task of Work, for any time exceeding four hours from the hour of Breakfast, on the morning next after admission.

AND PROVIDED ALSO THAT such amount of Work shall not be required from any person to whose age, strength, and capacity, it shall appear not to be suited.

Signed *Thos. Newbold*

Clerk to the Guardians.

WE, the POOR LAW COMMISSIONERS, do consent to, and approve of, the above Order of the Board of Guardians of the *Shardlow* - Union.

Dated this *Fourteenth* day of *May* — One thousand eight hundred and forty-*four* .

NOTICE.

Any such person as above who shall, while in such Workhouse, *refuse* or *neglect* to perform such task of work suited to the age, strength, and capacity of such person, will be deemed an *idle* and *disorderly* person, and be liable to be *imprisoned* in the House of Correction, with hard labor *for One Calendar Month.*

Discipline at Shardlow workhouse 1844

showed very strongly the middle class farmer and employer base of the social group from which were drawn the local overseers and operators of the new Poor Law.

The early Victorians who legislated changes in the Poor Law introduced a degree of centralisation and day-to-day governmental control quite new to Britain. The Poor Law Amendment Act of 1834 produced a structure of Commissioners, appointed in the first place for five years, with their appointment renewed for three successive years.[7] The Commissioners' initial lack of public accountability was rectified by the creation in 1847 of a Poor Law Board, with premises in Whitehall and answerable to Parliament through the Board's head – a President, who was an M.P. and a Member of the Government.[8]

Included in the countrywide structure of Union Boards were Shardlow, Loughborough, Ashby and Burton. They remained until political and administrative change had centralised welfare provision in Whitehall – presaging the day that the elderly and infirm might no longer be cast out.

Among the thirty-three parishes of the original Shardlow Union were eight contained in the area of the South Derbyshire District of 1974. Shardlow Union, established in 1844, was given administrative boundaries superimposed upon an ancient county structure, and comprising elements of Derbyshire, Nottinghamshire and Leicestershire. A wide swathe of Derbyshire land was covered by the Burton Union opened on 3 December 1843. County and Union boundaries did not coincide and matters were further complicated by the existence of detached portions of Derbyshire. In the case of inmates of Ashby Workhouse born in Appleby or Measham, the 1851 census suggested doubt as to their county of origin.

BREAKDOWN BY PROFESSION OF SHARDLOW UNION POOR LAW GUARDIANS, 1852[9]

Farmers	42	Brewer	1
Farmers/tanners	1	Lace manufacturer	1
Farmers/graziers	3	Cloth manufacturer	1
Farmers/ victuallers	1	Merchant	1
Gentlemen	2	Agent	1
Innkeepers	2		1

FANNY PEACE – A QUESTION OF INTERPRETATION

The Peace family, including Fanny, were residents of South Derbyshire within the authority for relief of the Burton on Trent Union. Hers was a case of disability, where the father, rather than have her sent to the workhouse, had applied for out-relief, citing loss of earnings resulting from her disability. The Poor Law Amendment Act of 1834, which had been designed to reduce out-relief to the barest minimum, had provided for the temporary continuance of such relief where there were adequate medical grounds. The case of Fanny, represented by her father, was based on medical considerations. The question was whether the Board would accept evidence produced by Jarvis Peace as being adequate within the meaning of the Act.

The circumstances of the case were examined by an Inspector appointed by the Poor Law Board, both parents were interviewed and the Board had before them a letter – notably literate, one might say – from the father.

The Board's eventual decision seemed to depend on whether total loss of earning power arising from disability would be required for an applicant to qualify for out-relief or whether substantial loss would be accepted as grounds to act.

An application for out-relief:

"gentlem look at this case if you please Sarah Peace the Wife of Jarvis Peace i went to Bord of gardins on the 21 day

December i ask the charman if he Wole be so kind to give daughter a little Relefe for she is a cripple the Charman said how old is your daughter i said 16 years old then ther Charman and the gaurdins [said] if you have kept the daughter until now you may keep her still on she as lost an hand and side I took a paper from the Doctor of the parsh that she was past all labour but i receved a Buseif [abusive] Discorse from the Bord guardins Charman the Governor wanted to put out Room the Reliven officer said she should not be Releved I have a wife and 6 children it is not posseable for me to mintain them out a Bougt 8 shilling a week."[10]

Jarvis Peace Newhall Derbyshire

H.B. Farrall, the Board's witness to the proceeding on 15 January 1849, had an interesting contribution on the attitude to the enquiry of Fanny Peace's mother who had been "attentively listened to by the Guardians on coming before them and was kindly and quietly spoken to by the Chairman" but had repaid this 'kindness' by "expressing herself unduly" and then refusing the relief offered to her daughter "without the slightest respect to the Guardians." An applicant a century later would no doubt have benefited from the assistance of a professional person before a tribunal able to call its own witnesses. Mr. Farrall, unsurprisingly, concludes that the Guardians' decision was 'just'.

BURTON UNION: QUALIFICATION FOR RELIEF

William Coxon, Chief Clerk to the Burton Union, writes to the Poor Law Board on 11 January 1849, concerning Fanny:

I am directed to inform you that the Pauper and her mother appeared before the Board on the 21st December last, that at the same time your Inspector H.B.Farrell Esq. was present and acquiesced in the decision of the Board which was an offer to relieve the said Fanny Peace in the Union

Workhouse.

The said Jarvis Peace hath five other children living with him. He was earning 2s/6d per day and the eldest of the said five Children was also earning 1s/0d per day, so that the family were in the Receipt of £1-1s/0d per week.

The charge made by Peace of unkind treatment and harsh language either from the Chairman, the Board, or their officers, is untrue.

Fanny Peace has not "lost a Hand and Side". There is a deformity of the Hand and Side which does not entirely preclude her from some kind of employment.

The Board having been informed that Peace had left his employment recently, relieving Officer was directed to enquire the cause before I replied to your letter he has seen the employer and reports that Peace has been discharged for neglecting his Work.

And further, from the way which in the family are brought up at home, the Board would, under any circumstances, decline relieving the girl out of the Workhouse.

I remain, Sir, your very
obedient Servant.
W. Coxon.
Clerk to the Board.

W.P.Lumsley Esq.,
Secretary to the
Poor Law Board.

SETTLEMENT AND EMIGRATION

The principle of settlement, indispensable to the early days of Poor Law, had created its own problems. Parishes could find their sometime meagre resources strained by seemingly endless obligations. With a reduction in the intensity of social strife (riots were possible; inhumanity had not gone away) but there were no more civil wars or ruinous repetitive campaigns against the Scots. Papist cells were no longer a threat to the Established Church. In such relatively favourable conditions movement of individuals became easier – but with due deference to the settlement laws. All local decisions were related to the effect on ratepayers of the funding parish.

EMIGRATION: A VESTRY MEETING IN SPONDON (SHARDLOW UNION)[11]

Decision: "It is resolved that the sum of £15 be forthwith raised by the Chirchwardens and Overseers as a fund or contribution for defraying the expenses of the emigration of poor persons having settlement in this parish, and being willing to emigrate, to be paid out of the rates raised or to be raised for the relief of the poor in this parish, and to be applied under such rules, orders or regulations as the Poor Law Commissioners for England and Wales shall in that behalf direct. And the said Churchwardens and Overseers were directed by the said meeting to raise such a sum of £15 accordingly." 30 May 1838

"This is a true Extract from the Vestry Book of the parish".
A.A. Holden, Minister
Joseph Kerry, Churchwarden
Joseph Potter, Overseer

Hundred of Repton and Gresley, Payments to Overseers of the Poor. 1847 [12]

Parish township or hamlet	Population at 1841 census	Overseer of the poor	Monies paid to the overseer in the year ended 5 April 1847		
			£	s	d
SOUTHERN DIVISION					
Castle Gresley (H)	164	William Peace	7	10	$6^1/4$
Cauldwell (H)	153	Samuel Tomlinson	8	12	$8^1/4$
Church Gresley (T)	993	James Rowley	25	13	$2^1/4$
Coton in the Elms (T)	351	Thomas Goodall	3	15	$2^1/4$
Linton (T)	253	John Fletcher	7	12	5
Newton Solney	311	William Tower	14	8	$5^1/4$
Repton (X)	2241	do	88	17	$1^1/2$
			5 April 1847		
NORTHERN DIVISION					
Hilton (T)	423	illegible	26	18	5
Barton Blount	68	Langley Wall	4	9	-27
Etwall	689	Dickenson Ward	27	7	$5^1/4$
Findern	416	Isaac Lovatt	30	15	$5^1/4$
Sutton on the Hill (T)	136	Thomas Pakeman	4	1	6
Willington	409	Gilbert Bull	11	5	7
			27 May 1847		

T = Township

H = Hundred

X = Repton parish includes Bretby (population in 1841: 298).

Note also that in Repton there was an extra influx of people in 1841 for a village wake, with stalls, games and displays, the artists and at least some of the visitors adding to the normal Easter total.

The new regime was founded upon Victorian principles of sobriety, work and religion in which the workhouse chaplain arranged and led the inmates in prayer. He conducted services for them either in the chapel or in an outside church. There was opportunity for ministration among the single mothers forming a substantial part of the workhouse population, typically surrounded by texts on the white-washed walls of their dormitories and dining areas. An essential part of the enforcement of discipline came from segregation of the sexes – made urgent by the presence in the establishment of so many young women who had 'fallen'. It was predictable in this regard that all would not go smoothly and that there would be incidents. The inescapable fact of a young male member of staff residing in such a closed community invited the very sort of happening that fierce regulations were designed to avoid. His professional status immaterial, George Ordish, schoolmaster, was a man and, presumably, available.

BURTON WORKHOUSE – THE SCHOOLMASTER'S TALE

Statement by G.F. Ordish (received at Poor Law Commission, 10 February 1843) [13]

George Francis Ordish

I admit that Mary Alson, Mary Ann Watson and Selina Blackshaw came into my bedroom in July last about midnight. I was asleep when they came in, the noise they made woke me and Mary Ann Watson took hold of my hands and she came by the side of my bed but I do not recollect saying anything about her being tight laced. She did not get into bed nor was she on it more than a minute or two. I did not have connexion with her. I told them to go and they went. I did not mention it to the Master or Mistress, as I ought to have done.

Selina Blackshaw was cleaning the Porters Lodge on the morning or afternoon the Governor and Porter went to the Stafford Sessions, and when I was requested to sleep in the Porter's Lodge, and she mentioned about coming to my room in the night with the other girls and I told her she must have the Lodge cleansed and by the time the Porter turned, and she said she would come into the Lodge at night, and I said you will be afraid to come at night, and she said, do you think that I am afraid of you, you would not be the first man I have come to, it passed off until night – about 10 o'clock, I unlocked the first door and went to the door of the Receiving Ward, she was in Bed, she came out and followed me into the Lodge, and sat down on one Chair and I sat on another, we then undressed ourselves and went to bed together and I had connexion with her.

(Signed) G.F. Ordish.

There was an irony in the circumstances of the exchanges between schoolmaster and young females – inmates of an institution with an habitually intimidating regime – conducted in the absence of the Governor who was on duty at the Stafford Sessions. An incautious confidence, presumably, had led first to disclosure of the whole episode, then to confession by Mr. Ordish to the Guardians – and the inevitable end of his tenure: the form of words that his resignation had been accepted. There is no record of the girls' subsequent fortunes, but presumably they awaited with interest the arrival of the next young male teacher. The Poor Law Commission met on 10 February 1843 and accepted Mr. Ordish's personal statement as grounds for issuing a dismissal notice, to take effect from that date.

BURTON WORKHOUSE: PROBLEMS IN THE SCHOOL-ROOM, 10 NOVEMBER 1852

A young man, apparently well qualified to teach, might well

be intimidated by the atmosphere he found in the work-house schoolroom. James Young, schoolmaster, reports to the board of Guardians with a catalogue of intolerable difficulties. (Extract)[14]

"At 3 o'clock on Monday morning, a boy named Francis Astbury, aged about 11 years and above named, in concert with another boy named William Jenks, of Tamworth, aged 14 years, commenced a performance consisting of a series of extemporaneous dances, not only in the bedroom which adjoins mine, but upon the bodies of the sleeping boys, contained therein.

Twice I had to leave my room in darkness, and in cold redolent of night, for the purpose of checking this riotous conduct, in which attempt I was not successful until daylight, when I ascertained that the head and font of the disorder were the two boys mentioned above – namely Astbury and Jenks.

As punishment I gave these two lads two pounds of more than half picked Oakum, telling them that when they had finished it, I should give them 4 spats on the hand each, and then breakfast (which I calculated would be about 2 hours after ordinary time).

Jenks finished his Oakum about 12 o'clock, but Astbury did not finish his until 4 o'clock.

In the midst of other business, I entirely forgot his breakfast, until he had had his dinner, but directly I was aware of it I directed that he should have it. I had occasion to leave the school for a few minutes previous to taking tea. When I returned, Astbury had gone off, leaving his day's work untouched. I found him in the yard communicating with his mother, who was in the men's dining hall. I therefore redeemed my promise of the morning, by administering 4 trifling spats on the hand of Astbury with a piece of half inch+ "Europe" – but I did not in the case of Jenks."

Mr. Young, seeing he must leave his post, writes a personal letter to the Board of Guardians.[15]

11 November, 1852.

Gentlemen.

As I am of no earthly use here and, consequently not earning my Salary – And as my allegience to Mr. Phillips (the workhouse Governor) ended on Monday night.
I have the honour to request that you will be pleased to dismiss me – which you can effect by suspending me today and confirming my dismissal next Thursday for I can bear the insults no longer from the Boys (which I am obliged to put up with at present) without doing some of them serious damage.
As I have but 5s/7d in the world, I cannot afford to lose the little money now owing to me by dismissing myself. Ergo – I pray your help, most earnestly.

I have the honour to be, Gentlemen,
Your obedient Servant.

(Signed)   James Young.

THE CASE OF MR. JAMES YOUNG – THE GUARDIANS' VIEW

Mr. Coxon, Chief Clerk to the Burton-on-Trent Guardians writes under the heading <u>Misconduct of Schoolmaster</u> to the Poor Law Board in Whitehall:[16]

11 November 1852

My Lords and Gentlemen

I am directed by the Guardians to inform you that for some time past the said Schoolmaster hath appeared dis-satisfied with his position and very singular in his habits and mode of

104

conducting the businefs of the School … The Guardians sent for this Schoolmaster and informed him that they should not dismifs him until they were legally authorized to do so by your honourable Board, upon which he became very angry and showed such a degree of hatred and avengeful feeling towards the children that the Guardians were of opinion it was not desirable to compel him to remain with the Children.

I have the honour to
remain my Lords and Gentlemen

Your very obedt. Servant

W.Coxon

FROM WORKHOUSE TO FACTORY

The existence at Horninglow of a large pool of cheap labour was attractive to local industry. After the Poor Law Amendment Act, Messrs. Bridget (silk manufacturers) had expressed themselves as being eager to employ pauper females preferably 'of the age of eleven years and upwards'. Deciding factors had been the consequences of the recent legislation and 'the deficiency of children which the alteration of the Factory Law had created': the words of the Clerk to the Burton Union.[17] With one ear to expressions of parliamentary displeasure in northern factories the Clerk to the Burton Union had begun by making the point that his workhouse's district was overwhelmingly rural; hence the attractiveness of an offer of employment by a large industrial concern that could offer board and lodging to workhouse girls. But looking at the history of these young workers from South Derbyshire and Staffordshire, one is struck by their extreme vulnerability: the first with a mother absconded; others orphaned and one with her mother in (another part of) the workhouse, but labelled a bastard.

ORPHANS INTO INDUSTRY, 1845

Jane Wilkins, aged 12 years, settlement Burton upon Trent, mother absconded and reported to be remarried.

Emma Barratt, 11, settlement Burton upon Trent, an orphan.

Mary Sutton, Do., Do., Do.

Millicent Jackson, 12, settlement Hilton, a bastard child, deserted by its mother.

Mary Ann Leech, 11, settlement Osbaston and Thurmaston, deserted by father, mother dead.

Mary Flackett, 11, a bastard child, mother in the workhouse.

'The first five have no parents to whom application could be made for the consent to the arrangement. The mother of the last, who is in the workhouse, without hesitation consented, and expressed a pleasure in the child being sent.'[18]

In proposing the arrangement to send young girls to the Derby factory, Burton Union cited the 'general difficulty in procuring employment for female labour in the rural parishes'.[19] Burton's Board laid much stress on safeguarding the girls' moral welfare by enlisting the help in Derby of the local Church.

TEXTILE WORKERS AND THE STRUGGLE TO SURVIVE

Textile workers in Derbyshire in the last quarter of the 18th century lived precariously on low wages that were declining and often fell below subsistence levels. By 1777, their wages had fallen to 10s to 12s a week on plain cotton and worsted hosiery and to 10s to 14s on silk goods. What the knitters earned by their labour might be very different from what they received. The frameworks knitters of Derbyshire, Leicestershire and Nottinghamshire petitioned Parliament unnecessarily to legislate on their behalf. Frames on which knitters worked in their homes were often rented: their evidence included statistics of how earnings fell drastically due to expenses earnings and stoppages, showing that an adult in 1777 might earn;[20]

	s.	d.	
at 12 pair worsted hose	7	0	per week:
Of which frame rent ..	0	9	
Standing room	0	3	
Needles	0	4	
Pulling worsted out ready for work	0	2	
Fire and candles	0	5	
Seaming	0	7	
	2	6	
	4	6	wage

Wages were inevitably depressed by the large numbers of women and children employed in textile trades who could more easily than men be intimidated or exploited by employers. Eden quotes children aged seven to twelve in Derby before 1800 who were paid 1s to 2s 6d per week in silk and cotton mills.[21]

In 1845, Felkin reported, wages of framework knitters 'rarely exceeded six or seven shillings a week, making it impossible for a man to maintain a family'.[22]

EDUCATING THE DEPRIVED

The establishment of a body of workhouses in the first half of the 19th century signalled the acceptance by government of responsibility for those without resources. The workhouse environment, despite its being intentionally deterrent, contained an educational component. This was introduced into a society where, until now, there had been systematic education only for the few. It is important to look at the motives of those who shaped the schooling of workhouse children, for instance, of those sent from Burton to the silk-works at Derby and who went to the schoolroom at the end of their day. The curriculum was intended to be moral, positive and relevant to the pauper girls' proper place. Their lessons would comprise 'reading, writing and the rudiments of arithmetic, sewing, knitting and singing; and a <u>knowledge of household domestic duties will be daily inculcated</u>. It is the want of this latter knowledge so common among factory operatives that is the greatest evil of the factory system'. (The text and underlining came from Mr Coxon, Clerk to the Burton Union).[23]

It could be said on behalf of both workhouse and factory schools that they were supplying children with a degree of literacy denied to the majority of their peers. A Poor Law Board administered the machinery to further the wishes of parliament and a Committee of Council on Education, with an address in Downing Street, met to determine the salaries appropriate for teachers in the new schools. James Young after meeting problems of discipline resigned from the Burton Workhouse and moved to a probationer post in the local Parochial Union School. For teaching a class of 26 pupils, he was paid £26 per annum, whilst Fanny Hanson, who had left the workhouse school at the same time – possibly out of sympathy with his position – was a colleague again in the new school. For teaching 20 pupils, she was paid £19 per annum. Against both teachers, it was recorded in the inspector's annual report that the 'state of the school' had not improved. This, translated, indicated that pupils had not performed well, at his annual visit, in answering the inspector's questions. Operating through a procedure of payment by results, salary levels responded to pupil performance.

It is of interest, in evidence collected by David Hillier, that the Inspector serving both Burton and Ashby, H.G. Bowyer, had criticised some aspects of the work of Sarah Stanley, schoolmistress at the Ashby-de-la-Zouch Union workhouse, who nevertheless continued to receive from him annual certificates of competence. To her salary of £25 had to be added 'board, lodging and washing', as listed in the advertisement for her post. When a new Inspector, Bryan Davies, was appointed to the Ashby Union, he produced a series of reports on Miss Stanley's teaching, the tone of which would lead in 1884 to her resignation. Mr. Davies had in that year written to the Ashby Union Guardians, saying that the teacher was 'quite incompetent to instruct the children properly' and, as a final blow, the Local Government Board stopped her last month's salary.[24]

The roll of workhouse children at Burton in 1847 shows far more boys than girls deserted by their parents, with fathers having been much more culpable. The figures for 1844 show more equality of suffering between boys and girls but the statistics are the result of the vagaries of nature and frailty, with the most important circumstance being the poverty from which the children had come. Hillier[25] shows that of workhouse children in Ashby born between 1851 and 1881, the proportion of them in every decade recorded as having been orphaned or deserted ranged from 28 per cent to 55 per cent. For the same period, the proportion of illegitimate children accompanied in Ashby workhouse only by their mother ranged from 33 per cent to 78 per cent.

The presence in both Ashby and Shardlow workhouses of former textile workers relates to problems in rapidly changing trades. Technology had added bigger enterprises whilst families working from home often found it difficult and expensive to adapt. Everywhere, prices were driven down from what had already been low levels. Framework knitters' earnings by 1845 had shrunk to 6s to 7s per week,[26] so that savings were not possible against the chance of even harder times.

Men were driven south from the Derwent Valley to Derby, but in that city there were instances of two or three operatives having to work in turns on new rotary machines that were kept running 18-20 hours a day.[27]

CIRCUMSTANCES OF CHILDREN
LEFT IN THE BURTON WORKHOUSE

CHILDREN IN THE WORKHOUSE	BOYS				GIRLS			
	Under 3 years Old	3 years Old and under 7	7 years Old and upwards	TOTALS	Under 3 years Old	3 years Old and under 7	7 years Old and upwards	TOTALS
Illegitimate,—their Mothers in the Workhouse	5	8	2	15	4	6	2	12
Illegitimate,—their Mothers not in the Workhouse	.	2	3	5	.	.	6	6
Children of Widows who are in the Workhouse	.	1	.	1	.	1	3	4
Children of Widows who are not in the Workhouse	.	.	.	.	.	.	.	.
Children of Widowers who are in the Workhouse	.	.	1	1	.	.	.	.
Children of Widowers who are not in the Workhouse	.	1	.	1	.	.	.	.
Children whose Father and Mother are dead	.	1	7	8	.	.	5	5
Children deserted by Father	1	3	2	6	.	1	.	1
Children deserted by Mother	.	.	2	2	.	.	.	.
Children deserted by both Parents	.	.	.	.	.	1	.	1
Children whose Father is transported, or suffering imprisonment for crime	.	1	.	1	.	.	2	2
Children whose residence in the Workhouse is caused by the bodily or mental infirmity of their Father or Mother	.	.	1	1	.	1	.	1
Children of able-bodied Parents who are in the Workhouse	.	.	.	.	.	.	.	.
Children of able-bodied Parents who are not in the Workhouse	.	.	.	.	.	.	.	.
Children not falling within any of the foregoing Classes	.	.	2	2	.	.	2	2
TOTALS	6	17	20	43	4	10	20	34

NOTE.—No Child is to be entered more than once, though such Child might fall within more than one Class.

Summary of Children in the Workhouse.

Boys.......... 43
Girls.......... 34
TOTAL. 77

PRO MH 12-11235

Signed this 19th day of March 1847.

_____, Clerk to the Guardians.

RECEIVED MAR 22 1847

110

Former Workers in Textiles, 1851 Workhouse Census – Distribution by Age and Settlement[28]

Branch of textiles	Ashby Union			Shardlow Union		
	Age	Settlement	Sex	Age	Settlement	Sex
Lace	37	Ticknall	F	34	Ilkeston	F
runner	31	Measham	F	36	do	F
	22	Donisthorpe	F	27	Dale Abbey	F
	38	Sawley	F	25	do	F
Silk factory man	35	Melbourne	M			
Wool framework			62	Spondon		M
knitter			51	Melbourne		M
Cotton spinner	34	Overseal	F	43	Measham	F
	54	Netherseal	F			

Analysis by Occupation of Workhouse Inmates (1851 Census)[29]

Rank, profession or occupation	Ashby	Burton	Shardlow
Textile workers			
Calico	1		
Wool	4		5
Lace	7		6
Silk	1		
Cotton	4	1	
Factory Women		1	7
Labourers			
Agricultural	21	13	7
Boatmen		1	5
Other labourers			2 x
Domestic servants (including charwomen and 'household workers')	18	36	15
Scholars (aged 4+)			
Boys	31	34	41
Girls	10	8	19
Infants (aged 1-3)			
Boys	3	8	3
Girls	5	4	2
Colliers	3		
Artisans	10	8	4
Members of professions	2		3

Statistics for Union Parishes in South Derbyshire
x One of Shardlow's former labourers had worked in a brickyard; another on the railway.

There were significant numbers of former farm labourers in the three workhouses, many of them elderly: farming may have been a healthy life, but was poorly rewarded. The work-houses held more boys than girls, suggesting a market for daughters to labour as young domestic servants. At Shardlow there were children, nearly all of them on their own, but else-where many children with their unmarried mothers. Attitudes common at that time held that to have produced a child out of wedlock was worthy only of censure, and there was official concern that girls at the workhouse would be contaminated by the presence of harder women with 'bastard' children. Ann Adams, a servant woman from Repton had arrived at Burton with three children, two born in Swadlincote and one in Church Gresley. Five girls from Newhall's Tilley family had joined the same workhouse leaving their parents at home, whilst Fanny Peace, also from Newhall, appeared in the same 1851 Horninglow register, her father Jarvis having applied unsuccessfully for out-relief on Fanny's behalf. Sarah Taylor of Measham, unmarried was in the workhouse with her two children.

Other casualties of the day included boatmen from Shardlow, (an area affected by the decline in canal business in a 'railway age') an 18 year-old collier from Measham, Melbourne's 'silk factory man' (35), and a schoolmaster from Barrow-on-Soar aged 25.

All of these people were in need: recently unemployed, elderly retired, and many mothers with children but no accompanying man. The assorted inmates had been classed as individuals to whom a duty of surveillance was owed, provided that it did not cost too much. The workhouse, emanating from within the Poor Law, carried an essential element of disapproval by the better-off. Treatment within it had to be such as to deter other able-bodied members of the poor. Fanny Peace's case was typical of early Victorian rules, where an expert supplied by the Board had despatched her to Horninglow, in the absence of representation on her

CENSUS RETURN OF BURTON-ON-TRENT UNION WORKHOUSE, 1851 (EXTRACT)[30]

Persons abiding here on the night of 31 March 1851	Relation to head of family	Condition	Age M	Age F	Rank profession or occupation	Where born
Workhouse Staff						
Alexander Phillips	Hd	Mar	53		Workhouse Master	Scotland
Jane	Wife			55	Workhouse Mistress	do
Richard	Son		19			Middx. St Pancras
William Graham			23		Schoolmaster	Stafford
Fanny Hanson				17	Schoolmistress	Derbys., Repton
John Davidson			50		Porter	Staffs. Burton-on-Trent
Jane Phillips	Dau			21	Dressmaker	Middx. St Pancras
Inmates						
Ann Adams #	Hd	Un		49	Servant	Derbys., Repton
Jane #				10	Scholar	do. Swadlincote
George #			7			do. do
Fanny #				3		do. Church Gresley
Elizabeth Ling		Un		39	Servant	do. Burnaston
John Lovatt		Un	31		Labourer	do. Findern
John Maddon		Un	41		Labourer	do. Repton
Joseph Mason		Un	46		Labourer	do. Lullington
Oscar Matthews			11		Scholar	do. Mickleover
Sarah Meakin		Un		55	Servant	do. Repton
William Mury				29	Labourer	not known
Emma Orme	Hd	Un		26	Servant	Derbys., Rosliston
Elizabeth Ling				6		do. Stapenhill
Ann Payne		Un		33	None	not known
Fanny Peace #		Un		17	None	Derbys., Newhall
Susannah Port	Hd			22	Mill hand	not known
John Riley			7		Scholar	Staffs. Sudbury
Thomas Riley			5		Do	do. Tutbury
Philip Roberts		Widr	82		Labourer	Derbys., Cubley
Sarah Taylor	Hd	Un		24	Needlewoman	Leics., Measham
Mary Ann				6		Staffs. Burton-on-Trent
William			2			do. do
Ann Tilley #				16		Derbys., Newhall
William #			15			do. do
Mary #				13	Scholar	do. do
Thomas #			9			do. do
Elizabeth #				6		do. do
William Tipper		Un	18		Labourer	Staffs. Rolleston
Charles Turner	Hd	Widr	69		Screw forger	do. Burton-on-Trent

Hd = Head of Family   Widr = Widower

Un = Unmarried   # = Mentioned in text

Dau = Daughter   Mar = Married

behalf. The Tilley family had to be penalised in the general interest for the inadequacy of the parents. Poor House inmates who were not extricated would in the end receive only the indignities of a pauper's funeral, and the institution would remain as a warning to the poor.

WORKHOUSE FOOD

Burton Union Board of Guardians, report of exchanges between Workhouse Master and members of Union Board.

Mr. Pickering: This morning one of the women brought a piece of bread and butter to me, and said she could not eat it. She also complained that the rice in the pudding was not half done, and as to the potatoes she could not even peel the dirt off.

A Member: When we were going round we remarked on the good quality of the bread, and in answer to our questions, the inmates said they were very comfortable.

Mr. Ward: The Master ought to hear this.

The Master was then called into the room.

Mr. Pickering reported his statement, and said he was told by inmates that they were starving, because they could not eat the food: it was not properly cooked, and was not good.

Mr. Taylor: Was that good bread which I showed you about a fortnight ago?

The Master: Well, that was a little bit off.

The Chairman: What do you mean?

The Master: It was sour and smelt a little bit.

Mr. Blakesley: I saw several loaves cut in two, and they were good.

The Chairman: We shall never see anything bad on Saturday morning.

Mr. Horne: The bread I saw was sour.

The Master stated, in answer to a question that the bread baked on Monday lasted till Saturday.

Mr. Massey believed there was a resolution on the books

that bread be baked three times a week in the summer and twice in the winter.

The Clerk said that was so.

The Rev. C. T. Moore: What about the dirt on the potatoes?

Mr. Pickering: Well, they were not properly cooked or the dirt would have come off. (Loud laughter).

The Chairman: We must use common sense, and see that bread is baked three times a week if we have passed such a resolution. (Hear, hear).

The matter then dropped.

Burton Mail August 8 1898.

1 Gregg, Pauline, A social and economic history of Britain 1760-1980, Harrap: London, 1982, p. 186.
2 Webb, Sidney & Beatrice (eds.), Minority Report of the Poor Law Commission, 2 vols., Longmans, 1909, p. 22.
3 TNA (PRO) MH12-11235
4 TNA (PRO) MH 12-2060
5 General order on workhouse rules (1841) – English Historical Documents, Vol. XII, pp. 725-6, British Library.
6 TNA (PRO) MH. 11233.
7 Gregg, op. cit., p. 183.
8 Ibid.
9 TNA (PRO) MH dated 13 April 1852.
10 Jarvis Peace, Newhall, Derbyshire, TNA (PRO) MH.12, 11234.

11 TNA (PRO) MH12-2060.
12 TNA (PRO) MH12-11234.
13 TNA (PRO) MH12-11235.
14 TNA (PRO) MH12-11235.
15 TNA (PRO) MH12-11235.
16 TNA (PRO) MH 12-11235.
17 TNA (PRO) MH12-11235.
18 TNA (PRO) MH12-11233.
19 Ibid.
20 VCH Derbys. Vol. II, p. 369.
21 Eden, op. cit. Vol. II, p. 129.
22 Felkin, W., History of machine-wrought hosiery, Com. Journal
    no. xxxvii, 1867, pp. 117, 457-60; in VCH Derbys. Vol. II, p. 369.
23 TNA (PRO) MH 12-11233.
24 Hillier, Kenneth, The Welfare and Education of working-class children
    in Ashby-de-la-Zouch in the Nineteenth Century (to 1980), Dissertation
    for the Degree of MA in English Local History, 1996, pp. 48-50.
25 Ibid., p. 52.
26 VCH Derbys. Vol. II., p. 369.
27 Ibid.
28 TNA (PRO) HO/107.
29 TNA (PRO) HO/107 2084, 2012 (Burton) 2140
30 TNA (PRO) HO 107/2140.

CHAPTER 8

MANAGING THE MENTALLY ILL

Among the most vulnerable people in need of poor relief were the mentally ill. A Select Committee of the House of Commons, meeting in 1807 and charged with examining the condition of "pauper lunatics", had properly concluded that the treatment of those boarded out in private mad-houses depended 'wholly upon the good conduct of the keeper'[1] – a point particularly relevant to those counties like Derbyshire, where nothing had been achieved towards publicly-run specialist relief. Destitute lunatics were in effect chattels in what Parry-Jones identified as a trade in lunacy. An asylum keeper, as the Commons committee reported, would probably also be the owner, conducting the business for profit. He would be under no obligation to report admissions to the College of Physicians (who would have been expected to be interested in the adequacy of arrangements in the madhouse). The inadequacy of the inspections required of the statutory Commissioners of Lunacy was demonstrated by the fact that their remit did not insist on an examination of the inmates' conditions.[2]

The national conscience was increasingly disturbed by details seeping out from the different institutions with pauper lunatic inmates. Solutions were impeded by the prejudices of influential men such as John Scott, first Earl of Eldon, Lord Chancellor and the declared enemy of all liberals. 'Philanthropists' were famously described by Eldon as 'men pretending to humanity but brimful of intolerance and swollen with malignity'.[3] Opposition such as his helped explain the delay in constructing a national system of asylums. Lunacy Commissioners in 1830 said that large buildings were urgently needed 'fitted up expressly'[4] but it was not until 1845 that every county was ordered by

Parliament to build its own asylum.

For a long time government had had to acknowledge the existence of pauper lunatics, whether or not a danger to themselves or others, whom poverty had driven into an institution – there, to require maintenance at the ratepayer's expense. For the individual lunatic, there had until 1845 been lamentably little chance of his receiving any help appropriate to his needs.

PAUPER LUNATICS: COST OF MAINTENANCE[5]

1839 estimates (national figure)

Category of accommodation	Shillings per week per inmate / per individual
Paupers in asylums	8 / -
Paupers in workhouses	3 / -
Patients in private asylums	20 / -
Criminals in jails	3 / -

Tuke's figures were derived from the global sums that had been collated by the Lunacy Commissioners and bear interesting comparison with Derbyshire maintenance levels: Commissioners' national weekly estimates for 1839 of 8s were little different from the 9s chargeable to Melbourne and Shardlow parishes for pauper lunatics sent to the newly-opened Derbyshire County Asylum[6] during the period 1853-9. But as anti-reformers in Parliament had known, it cost much more to keep victims, however inadequately, in asylums than it did in workhouses.

It was the heroic achievement of D.H. Tuke to do more than any other in first investigating and then illuminating the price of neglect by society of the mentally impaired. His most telling evidence was directed against what was euphemistically called restraint, whereby unfortunates, unseen and unknown, could be fettered, beaten and abused. The evils diminished as public opinion ensured that Parliament was alerted and a system of Visitors organised.

Derby County Lunatic Asylum 1853

By the time that the Metropolitan Lunacy Commissioners reported in 1844, the situation had materially improved, though not everyone would have been entirely reassured by the Commissioners' conclusion that "the safeguards against lunatic patients being subject to harsh or unnecessary restraints from cruelty, idleness or caprice of their attendants have been multiplied."[7]

There remained the matter of the private asylums, of which nine 'provincials houses' in various parts of the country outside London were reported by the 1844 Commissioners as deserving "almost unqualified censure": one of them, Derby's Green Hill House.

Workhouses generally were not well equipped to deal with inmates, or patients, given to fits or 'seizures'. Still less could they cope with those who were seriously disturbed. Much of course would depend on the quality of diagnosis, especially in the early stages, by the resident medical officer, who presumably would have welcomed the possibility of referral or transfer to an establishment with fuller facilities. From the middle of the century, it became an option for Medical Officers in the community to dispatch a case direct to an asylum, provided only that this could be financed by the parish.

119

The Shardlow Union records cases of varying severity for the period of 1871-3:

1. The workhouse had been able to cope with a man afflicted with 'epileptic madness'.

2. Transfer to the Derby asylum was effected for a woman reported as being habitually violent, given to 'foul languages' and the singing of 'obscene songs'. It had required three women staff to restrain her with the aid of 'towels'.

3. This case, leading to an inquest, concerned a middle-aged woman who had set fire to herself before admission and she had died in the workhouse. Returning a verdict of accidental death, the jury added a rider that a doctor's opinion should have been sought rather than that of an Overseer of the Poor. A doctor's direction, said the jury, could have produced the 'alleviation' that did not occur. The workhouse, it added, could not be faulted in the treatment offered to the woman, but critically, there had been a lack of 'appropriate procedures' undertaken before admission.[8]

Two Commissioners for Lunacy visiting the Shardlow Workhouse in 1852 found that there was no 'lunatic ward or room set apart for the idiots and the bedding or clothing of that class are the same as those for the general body of the inmates', that the house stood 'on the roadside a short distance from the village of Shardlow on the Derby side', and that its grounds included three acres of gardens. Most of the lunatic inmates were women – and there was a marked range of ages among the inmates of both sexes, with one very elderly lady having evidently returned from the asylum to spend the last of her sad days in the workhouse.

LUNATICS IN SHARDLOW WORKHOUSE – REPORT OF 22 JULY, 1852 [9]

Males		Females	
Condition	Age	Condition	Age
Idiot	34	Imbecile	26
Imbecile	30	I 'has been in that state for many years	47
Do	20	I	27
'Tending idiotic'		11 Do	27
		Do	26
		Do	23
		Do	18
		Do 'has been at Nottingham asylum'	84

Contemporary definitions: Imbecility = mentally deficient
Idiocy   = behavioural disorder resulting
from mental deficiency

PAUPER LUNATICS CHARGEABLE TO A PARISH – MELBOURNE [10] (SHARDLOW UNION, 1 JAN. 1851)

Pauper's name	Age	Lunatic or idiot	Residing with	Dangerous or not to self or others	Weekly cost of maintenance & clothing	For what length of time supposed to be of unsound mind
Elizabeth Pilkington	60	Lunatic	Daughter in Aston near Birmingham	No	2/0	9 years
Mary Shaw Newton	68	Idiot	Sister at King's	No	2/4¼	From birth
Priscilla Smith	39	Idiot	w. sister at Melbourne	No	2/4¼	From birth

<u>Later definitions</u>: 'Lunatic' = mentally ill; 'Idiot' = someone with a personality disorder/learning difficulties.

DECISIONS ON PLACEMENT OF SOUTH DERBYSHIRE LUNATICS[13] (SHARDLOW UNION 1861-2)

Pauper's name and parish chargeable	Age	Lunatic, idiot etc	Future residence (w – retained in workhouse)	Dangerous or not to self or others	Weekly cost of maintenance & clothing	Number of years supposed to be of unsound mind
Ellen Bakewell (Melbourne)	43	Lunatic	To Derby County Asylum 14 Dec 1853	Yes	9/0	20 years
Charles Hatton	16	Idiot	With sister in Melbourne	No	1/11	From birth
Fanny Helmsley (Melbourne)	31	Lunatic Asylum	To Derby County	Yes	9/0	Unknown
Amos Pass (Melbourne)	22	Lunatic	To Derby County Asylum 18 March 1859	No	9/0	12 years
Mary Shaw (Melbourne)	77	Imbecile	W. sister in King's Newton	No	2/5	From birth
Reuben Sherrin (Shardlow)	27	Lunatic	To Derby County Asylum 10 Oct 1856	Yes	9/0	3 ½ years
Priscilla Smith (Melbourne)	49	Idiot	w	No	3/5	From birth
Rebecca Wivey	19	Idiot	w	No	1/11	From birth
Mary Wakefield	64	Idiot	With brother in	No	2/5	From birth
Stanton-by-bridge						

Green Hill House, Derby: private lunatic asylum.
From Glover's Directory 1843

By the provision of the Poor Law Amendment Act of 1844 the detention of dangerous lunatics and idiots in work-houses for longer than fourteen days was prohibited – a provision, says Parry-Jones,[11] difficult for a union to keep: the costs of maintaining pauper lunatics in a workhouse were often half what would be needed to keep an inmate in a private madhouse or county asylum. Moreover, however unsatisfactory conditions might be for the non-dangerous lunatic in the average workhouse, patients might well, in the censorious social climate of the time, be much safer inside than outside the workhouse walls.

GREEN HILL HOUSE, DERBY [12]
(private asylum)

"… the straw in the paupers' beds was found filthy, and some of the bedding was in a disgusting condition from

123

running sores, and was of the worst materials, and insufficient. Two cells, in which three sick epileptic paupers slept, were damp, unhealthy, and unfit for habitation. The beds of some of the private patients were in an equally bad state."

Extract from the report of the Metropolitan Commission in Lunacy, p. 56, quoted by William Lloyd Parry Jones.

With the programme of asylum-building in the mid-nineteenth century, pressure on a workhouse management combating inexperience and overcrowding began to ease. Since provisions covering mental health were applied on a county not Union basis, severe cases originating with natives of Shardlow village were in future to be sent to the Derbyshire (Mickleover) asylum, whilst Shardlow inmate-patients born, for instance, in Castle Donnington were despatched to the asylum opened in Leicester in 1837.

1 Jones, W.L.P., The trade in lunacy: a study of private madhouses in England in the eighteenth and nineteenth centuries, Routledge & Kegan Paul: London, 1972., p. 14.
2 Ibid.
3 Ibid., p. 16.
4 Ibid., p. 253.
5 Tuke, Daniel Hack, Chapters in the history of the Insane in the British Isles, Kegan Paul: London, 1882, p. 222.
6 TNA (PRO) MH 12 2067.
7 Tuke, op. cit. p. 223.
8 TNA (PRO) MO 12 2064.
9 Ibid.
10 Ibid.
11 Jones, op. cit. p. 19.
12 Ibid.
13 TNA (PRO) MH 12 2067.

CHAPTER 9

LAW AND ORDER

WORKHOUSE INMATES AND THE LAW

The commonest cause for an inmate to have encountered legal problems arose from the many unmarried mothers compelled to find sanctuary for themselves and their children. Such were Hannah Astbury of Willington who had conceived and borne two children in Walton-on-Trent – the first in 1843 – before entering the Burton Workhouse, and Emily Hollis of Rosliston, also a servant, who had had two children born in Burton – the second only two months before the 1851 census.

Mothers were under an obligation, by the Bastardy Act of 1733, to name the father of any child born out of wedlock. Guardians of the Poor of the Union – in these cases Burton-on-Trent – containing the parish in which the child was born, had then to pursue the named father, and attempt to serve papers on him.

A very different cause for legal involvement concerned the mother like Elizabeth Coates in 1836, whose husband had been transported to Tasmania, leaving a destitute family dependant upon the law's mercy.

SENTENCES OF TRANSPORTATION PASSED AT DERBY ASSIZES

	Male	Female
1827	3	-
1828	10	1
1829	10	3
1830	10	1
1831	2	2
1832	7	1

Francis Taylor, aged 17, *Robert Mozley*, aged 15, *Ann Yeomans*, aged 18, were charged with stealing one silk shawl, one tea caddy, two books, and sundry other articles. —And the said Ann Yeomans, charged with receiving the same knowing them to have been stolen.

Sarah Hibbert lives at Twyford, and during the night of the 9th October the various articles named were stolen from her house, the thieves got into the house by taking out a pane out of a window, and so opening the casement ; she did not see the things stolen until they were in Allen's possession. They were now produced and identified.

Ruth Almond and Sarah Staley (who were themselves indicted, for neglecting to enter into recognizance for their appearance at the Sessions, to give evidence against the prisoners) spoke to the articles stolen being concealed in Mr. Wilson's nursery, and to pawning the shawl at Mr. Lomax's for 9d ; the articles produced in court were those which they saw in the nursery.

Thomas Boultby, shopman to Mr. Lomax, deposed to the pawning the shawl, which was afterwards given up to Allen, constable.

Allen said he apprehended the prisoners, and at Yeoman's house he found the bible, tea caddy, and prayer book.

Thomas Fisher saw Mozley and Taylor begging on the 9th October in Twyford.

Guilty ; Taylor and Mozley of the robbery, and Yeomans of receiving the goods knowing them to have been stolen.— The two former were sentenced to 7 years transportation, and Yeomans to six month's imprisonment and hard labour.

STEALING FROM A SHOP IN THE IRONGATE.

Thomas Bentley, aged 14, was charged with stealing at the parish of All Saints, three sets of curls, the property of Thomas Hawkridge.

The prisoner was seen at the window of Mr. Hawkridge about 8 in the evening of the 14th of December, endeavouring by means of a wire to extract through a hole, the curls out of the window frame ; he had succeeded in obtaining two sets, and was detected in the third.—*Guilty ;* three months imprisonment, and hard labour, and to be once privately but severely whipped.

Transportation involved the operation between the colonies and the United Kingdom of a process of supply and demand for labour. Its basis was the statute of 4 Geo. I cap. 11. On 6 August 1720, an order addressed to Mr. Wilmot of Osmaston directed that Helen Martin, convicted of theft and larceny, was to be transported via the port of Liverpool – departure point for the American colonies.

The route to Liverpool was well-trodden, with convicts for tran-shipment being conveyed sometimes in a wagon, sometimes on horseback, accompanied by warders. The journey to Liverpool would be expected to take four days. An estimate from forwarding agents for taking eleven prisoners thus to Liverpool was for £20 18s 5d.[1]

After the American War of Independence and the Napoleonic wars, transportation routes were diverted to the Cape Colony of South Africa or Australia, where the most favoured landing point was Hobart, Van Diemen's Land (Tasmania): see the case of Edward Coates and also the earlier prisoner from Derby Gaol, who had left for the colonies via the *Ganymede* prison hulk.

DERBY GAOL: A PRISONER'S REPORT

A parliamentary enquiry in 1835 received replies from prisoners in various gaols to a questionnaire. In the case of a Derby inmate (unnamed), aged 41, he had been sentenced to seven years' transportation for "stealing a silk cloak and other articles".

After two days and nights in the reception room, where he saw the surgeon, he was ordered to the untried ward, with ten to eleven other prisoners. [A key question concerned 'Conduct and Conversation when Silence was not maintained'].

"... there was no Restraint as to Conversation, which was usually of the very worst Description, cursing, swearing, most profane and obscene talk, sometimes singing bad

Old Prison, Friar Gate, Derby, in use until 1840

Songs, sometimes quarrelling and fighting; they gambled and played at "Pitch and Toss"; there was seldom an officer present; he was appointed as a Wardsman, but dared not report any of the Prisoners for fear of their murdering him."

[In answer to the question as to whether the prisoner would prefer the discipline of silence to the danger of 'contamination' through 'communication', he is reported to have readily agreed. There is reason to doubt whether the vocabulary quoted was typical even of a model inmate, but it is reasonable to suppose that the prisoner who is quoted here, however inaccurately, feared his fellow-inmates and they in turn mistrusted him.]

"Friends were allowed to bring in Provisions, or Prisoners were permitted to purchase Food, Tobacco or Snuff, Porter or Ale (not exceeding 1 pint for each Person), but no Spirits; would prefer the Discipline and Silence of the Penitentiary to the unrestrained and contaminating Communication with other Prisoners as at Derby Gaol; could neither read nor write when received."

He further states that he was put on board the Ganymede hulk at Woolwich on the 15th January 1834, and was sent to the Penitentiary on the 6th of the following month.[2]

Behind the long programme of enquiry was a mood of great official uncertainty stimulated by a fashionable remedy of 'Silence' practised in other gaols and counties. Glover from his own observation inside Derby gaol criticised a situation where "young and old, untried and convicted, capital and petty offenders, sick and healthy, associate together throughout the day, and have the means of conversing during the night."[3]

Although the Poor Law Amendment Act prohibited the detention in the workhouse for longer than fourteen days of dangerous lunatics and idiots, in practice it became impossible to adhere strictly to this objective, owing to the expense of keeping lunatics in either a private madhouse or in a county asylum. There were further crucial difficulties for authorities lacking beds for such provision. There was also the practical problem for those new to this area of social concern in agreeing a definition of 'dangerous' lunatic.[4]

DERBY GAOL AND HOUSE OF CORRECTION, 1835[5]

Prisoners Held		Prisoners Under 17		Debtors
1833	1834	Male	Female	
20	34	6x	-	2 x

Punishments			
Whippings	Held in irons	Serving hard Labour	Receiving Solitary confinement
		19 x	17 xx
Occasions imprisoned previous to 1835			
Once	Twice	Three	Four or more
22	13	9	7

Cases of sickness during the year
91 xxx

x   included in total prisoners held
xx   three of these cells were below ground
xxx held in 'apartments provided for the sick, male or female'

Prisoners on a treadmill, 1825

PRISON ROUTINES, MEN

There were extremes of official regulation from the tending of plants in the prison garden to being worked to the point of exhaustion. For hard labour sentences, the standard punishment was the treadwheel. Having come off that contrivance, the prisoner would spend most of the day in either solitary confinement or a repetitive task.

WOMEN

The basic picking-of-oakum punishment could be leavened with other repetitive but less repellent tasks that included cleaning, washing and sewing.

SUNDAY PRISON ROUTINES, 1833

Asked to provide a job description the prison chaplain said that he read morning service in the prison chapel at 9 o'clock each morning (9.30 in winter) as well as visiting such prisoners as required his "further attention". On Sundays, Christmas Day and Good Friday, he conducted two services – one in the morning; the second in the afternoon, and after one of them visited the Sunday School attached to the prison. Rev. Pickering, assisted by a curate, was also responsible for the two churches of Mackworth, for which work he was paid "the annual value of the vicarage" – £161.[7]

TRANSPORTATION

Convicts sentenced to transportation at Derby Assizes, leaving wives and families resident in Burton Union.[6]

Surname	First Names (Wife Husband)	Name of colony where the husband is at present.	Date of conviction at Derby	Age of children Under 7		9-14		Over 14	
				M	F	M	F	M	F
Ashmole	Rhoda William	Lancaster, Van Diemen's Land	1826				1		
Coates	Elizabeth Edward	Not Known	1836	1	1	1			
Hind	Ann John	do	1834 (?)		1	1	1		
Jones	Mary Hugh	do	1838		1	2			
Woolley	Mary Joseph	do	1837			1			2

The wife and three children of Edward Coates entered the Burton Workhouse after his conviction. The families of the other four convicts were resident in the Burton-on-Trent Union.

DERBY GAOL AND HOUSE OF CORRECTION, 1833: SALARIES [8]

Name	Position	£	s	d
John Sims	Governor	360		
Mary Sims (his wife)	Matron	40		
John Thompson	1st Turnkey	52		
Thomas Mather	2nd	52		
Charles Birch	3rd	49	8	
Joseph White	4th	41	12	
Edward White	5th	41	12	
John Collins	night watchman	41	12	
Elizabeth Smith	Female turnkey	31	4	
The Rev. George Pickering	Chaplain	150		
Douglas Fox	Surgeon	100		

Dated 9 May, 1833 John Charge, Clerk to the Peace.

1 Cox, op. cit. Three Centuries of Derbys. Annals, Vol. II, p. 51.
2 Brit. Parl. Papers, 1835, Vol. 4, Crime and Punishment.
3 Glover, op. cit. Vol. II, p. 445.
4 Parry, op. cit. p. 19.
5 Brit. Parl. Papers, op. cit., p. 315 (Prisons).
6 TNA (PRO) MH 12 11233. Documents signed by William Coxon, Clerk to the Guardians, on 30 July 1846.
7 Ibid., p. 566.
8 Ibid., p. 596.

CHAPTER 10

EDUCATION AND IMPROVEMENT

When Sir John Port of Etwall died in 1567 he left a will setting up a grammar school, which he intended to be a place of learning. The Repton School site incorporated part of the remains of the Austin Canons priory.

The school was advertised both as helping families of quality to gain admission for their sons to Oxford and Cambridge and also offering a mixture of classes in the school's intake: "the sons of the village carpenter side by side with the son of the squire of high degree." One must not exaggerate this degree of 'education for all' and, in 1621, during a refoundation, just four 'poor scholars' (paying no fees) were specifically directed to be maintained at the school.[1]

In 1683, Richard Meynell who had moved to London to practise as an apothecary, left money both to the school and to the poor of the district:

"I give to the poore of the parish of Willington where my ancestors and myself were borne twenty shillings a year for ever to be issuing and payable out of the rents and proffits of the lands called Powke hole att Repton in the county of Derbyshire which lands to be settled to Willington as well as counsell shall direct to secure the said annual summe and I give towards the furnishing of the schoole and library lately erected there and for books for poore children five pounds."[2]

There was an increase in total numbers, and also in the free element. Foundation [poor] scholars increased to twenty but in 1824 their numbers were cut to eight. In 1832, the Marquess of Hastings and the Earl of Chesterfield directed through Parliament laws restricting free places, previously

Ashby-de-la-Zouch Grammar School as it was around 1880

available to all, to the sons of residents from Etwall and Repton.

When School Enquiry Commissioners reported on Repton in 1866, out of a total of 206, 26 were day boys, adding that Latin, Greek and Maths were taught to all; whilst French, drawing and music were optional subjects, requiring extra fees.[3]

At Ashby-de-la-Zouch, in Leicestershire, a short distance from the Derbyshire border, a grammar school had opened in 1567 using money and property transferred by the third Earl of Huntingdon. Statutes and orders dated 1575 were quoted to require that a schoolmaster applying for a post at Ashby was to be "Noe Papist nor Heretic," but "able to teach the Latin tongue".[4]

At Appleby Parva, then in Derbyshire, Christopher Wren built a grammar school that opened in 1697 – one wing and rooms over the school occupied by the headmaster and the boarders. It was (and is) a splendid building – and, in

135

Melbourne's National School, built 1738

Glover's words, "altogether a very suitable edifice and may serve as a model for others,"[5] apt words since in the 20th century it was to become a primary school standing in its original spacious grounds.

As to the interests of the lower orders in the 17th and 18th centuries; powerful voices were raised against universal education. No less an authority than Dr. Johnson held that if "teachers of good" and "propagators of bad" were allowed to compete, the inferior product would always win.[6]

Melbourne's National School, opened in 1738 was given a permanent endowment by Lady Elizabeth Hastings.[7] The

Moravians opened a school along with their large chapel at Ockbrook in 1750. But there was no general bursting of bonds; colliers' children, said the Hammonds, were denied entry to some Derbyshire National and Free schools.[8] In Parliament, both the Lord Chancellor and the Archbishop of Canterbury were among the great majority of peers defeating a Bill introduced by Samuel Whitbread in 1807 that would have given elementary education to all. But opinion, in this era of revolution in Europe and reform in Britain, was not immovable.

The merchant class saw some advantages in a literate workforce. The churches insisted that any legislation was morally based which, in translation, meant that any proposal, to gain government approval, would need to contain a strong and unequivocal religious element. Rival societies were soon busy, each promoting its own prospectus. One such body was founded in 1808, after a Bill giving local authorities the option of sustaining local elementary schools by levying a rate and providing the poor with two years' free education.[9] This first society, founded and patronised by Nonconformists, particularly Quakers, grew into the British and Foreign Schools Society. Competing with them and founded in 1811 was the National Society for Promoting the Education of the Poor in the Principles of the Church of England.

The existence of diehard opposition to the education of the most needy ensured that the planning picture was patchy. But enlightened local councils like that of Shardlow moved ahead. A Town Meeting on 22 June 1803, received a proposal concerning the 'great number of young children wholly neglected in being neither sent to a 'place of Public Worship,' nor given even some slight education for want of a proper place' on which to erect a school.

It was resolved that a suitable plot of land be sought, the expense to be met partly by public subscription, partly from a levy on those liable for payment of the Poor Rate. The school opened in 1810, with Frederick Timms, 'a profound scholar of Shakespeare', as its schoolmaster. The building was enlarged at a cost of £900 and re-opened in 1838 as a National School, with Mr. Timms still Master and Miss Alice Williams as Mistress. There was accommodation (though it was not for some time fully taken up) for 100 boys and 100 girls, plus an infants' department. The Master and Mistress each received £70 per annum in salary and a more lowly schoolteacher £15 a year.[10]

The precious attribute of literacy was the prize for those attending the National Schools. It mattered little to many parents whether it was to the Established or, further north in the county, the Nonconformist Church that their children's curriculum was orientated. However small the facilities, there was a vital cultural asset available for the parent making the necessary sacrifice.

Besides the National Day Schools there were the important denominational Sunday Schools. When blacksmith's daughter Ann Waring married collier George Peace at Coalville in 1855, they were both able to give a signature to the marriage certificate, their witness Henry Pointon appending his mark. In 1851, neither Edwin Hull nor his bride Elizabeth Jones had been able to sign at the ceremony in Gresley on 23rd November, nor had their witness, Grace Jones, but the bridegroom's cousin Isaac, the other witness, did sign. When Edwin Hull's son was sent to the Church Gresley Primitive Methodist Sunday School, he periodically practised his signature on the front page, having difficulty only with the spelling of his first name – Richard.

The revolution in production that affected for ever the working lives of those who lived by coal, clay or textiles – and the trades supplying them – helped complicate the opportunities for young people's schooling. Industrial progress could involve the exploitation of those in society who were most vulnerable. Reformers had drawn attention to the unacceptably long hours that had been worked by children in the colliery industry and Liberals were successful in alerting the public to the facts of average hours worked by children underground: twelve hours per day in Leicestershire and fourteen in Derbyshire. With the earliest average age at which children started work below ground being seven in Leicestershire and five to six in Derbyshire, it was not surprising when such pit children who attended day or Sunday school should show the effects of their labour. Commissioners reporting in 1842 on child labour in this region said about Thomas Straw, aged seven of Ilkeston:

> "They would not let him sleep in the pit, or stand still; he feels very tired when he comes out, gets his tea and goes to bed. Feels tired and sleepy and on a Sunday morning would rather be in bed than go to school."[11]

The sub-commissioner's report on the condition of the children working in the mines recorded the comments of William Hawley, schoolmaster of Ilkeston:

> "Has certainly perceived those children who work in the pits much more dull and stupid than the others both at school and chapel; it is his opinion children are at the pits too young, and it is decidedly too long for children to work from six to eight; he had often to complain of the colliers' children's bad attendance on Sunday mornings and the reply generally is they were so tired they overslept themselves."[12]

There were numerous parents who made sacrifices in the 1860s to enable their children to attend school. But there was a problem in reconciling the education of young scholars with the business demands of farmers for cheap young labour. The differential effect of the seasons on work and education was addressed by John Coleman, agent to the owner of the very large Kedleston estate. Boys, he said, who were taken on under the age of twelve and "have to go a part of the day at a busy time of the year to school, are of no use to the farmer, whose operations are carried on, as a whole generally, and therefore if the boys are absent, the whole machinery stops".[13]

The Hilton statistics, provided by Mr. George Lucas, the master of its endowed school, illustrated the problem of keeping regular attendance through the year, especially for boys over 10 years of age. However, the regime here was evidently more adaptable than in the more feudal atmosphere of Kedleston.

SCHOOL NUMBERS:

Register of the children of the 'agricultural labouring class' attending the Hilton endowed school (1867)[14]

	In Summer	
	On the register	Average attendance
Boys:		
Under 10	22	18
Between 10 and 13	14	5
Girls:		
Under 10	5	5
Between 10 and 13	2	2
	In Winter	
Boys:		
Under 10	30	24
Between 10 and 13	28	22
Girls:		
Under 10	7	7
Between 10 and 13	5	5

In the middle Trent valley villages (including Shardlow, where there was some industry, but wages were still low) parents had problems similar to those of the colliers and clayworkers further south. Could they afford to take up for their children such school places as became available? The fees, although they were low, represented a drain on small resources. The work of these schools showed what could be done by significant people of goodwill.

SCHOOLS OF THE MIDDLE TRENT VALLEY[15]

Township	Population (1861)	Status of school	Fee charged	Patron
Church Broughton	651	Free	1d-3d (i)	
Egginton	355	Endowed		Sir Henry Every
Elvaston (ii)	500		1d (2d winter night-school)	Earl of Harrington
Hilton	719	Endowed		

(i) At Church Broughton the fees charged were: 3d per week for the first child; 2d for two children and 1d for each of three children.

(ii) The patron, the Earl of Harrington, paid the school-master a salary of £65 per year, provided him with rent-free accommodation in the school house and also paid £8 per year to a girl to teach sewing.

The Forster Education Act of 1870 changed for all time the old division of society into the illiterate many and the literate few. It aimed to ensure that there were sufficient school places available for every child to attend but large families were often still disadvantaged in using the facilities that legislation appeared to offer to all. Joseph Payne, born in 1853, eventually became a manager of the governing school board of York Road School, Church Gresley. His daughter Maria, a very bright girl, benefitted from the Forster Act, attending York Road until the age of 12 and a half. Then economic necessity forced her father to take her out of school. With seven mouths to feed in the family Joseph was unable to accept the Head Teacher's offer to give

Maria Payne aged 11, third from left in second row of Grade 1, Girls'
Department, Board School, York Road, Church Gresley. 1892

© M. Hull

his clever daughter an extra year at school as a monitress.
Her wages were needed to help the family budget.

Limitations that affected labourers did not apply to new
members of the middle class in late Victorian England. Its
relatively privileged families could find for their children a
degree of private help to add on to state provision. At a
halfway point between Church Gresley and Swadlincote
stood the well regarded Mr Burton's Academy – its sessions
held in the clubroom of a beer shop in Hastings Road. Mr.
Burton's wife, a few doors away, conducted a school for girls
(fees 30s quarterly) teaching among other things
complicated needlework to pupils who had moved from
Board School, sometimes at the age of 12.[16]

For the better-off wishing further to extend the
opportunities for their children, grammar schools lay within
reach of South Derbyshire, bearing in mind the necessity to

142

A typical village school. Netherseal, early 20th century

By courtesy of C Liversuch

manage a journey to Burton-on-Trent or Ashby-de-la-Zouch. It required another Education Act in 1902 (promoted by A.J. Balfour) to make available public money to pay for entry through enabling grants to grammar schools. In Derby the local education administration, organised County Minor Scholarship examinations (known as the 10 plus) permitting labourers and artisans to have their children's fees paid.

TEACHING AND TEACHERS

Teachers in the early 19th century were important members of society, but rewards for those entering the profession were not high. A headmaster in 1850 could expect to be paid about £70 per annum and a teacher at the Shardlow Parochial School only £15.[17] Pay differentials were significant. In 1852, Fanny Hanson, starting at the Burton-on-Trent Parochial Union School was allotted £19 p.a., as against her colleague

A typical village school class. Findern c. 1905

James Young's £23 18s, the two teachers having been expected to offer their deprived pupils religious knowledge, spelling, penmanship, arithmetic, grammar, history and geography.

In 1863 a post was advertised for a schoolmaster at the Shardlow Workhouse paying £30 p.a.[18] The Ashby Workhouse had an advertisement placed by its Poor Law Union in 1875, for a schoolmistress vacancy paying £25 p.a.: the salary to be 'together with board, lodging and washing in the Workhouse'.[19]

In 1893 a post was advertised by the Church Gresley School Board:

'Wanted – 2 Assistants (Ex P.T.s, Male or Female) for Boys' Department. Average (number on roll) 210. Must be good disciplinarians and capable of teaching Drawing and Singing by rote (Tonic - sol - fa). Applications to Henry Orgill, Prospect House, Church Gresley'.[20]

SUNDAY SCHOOL IN 1892-3

Maria Hull, in her memoirs, described the impact made on the community by a Swadlincote Sunday school:

The Methodist (Free Church) Sunday School, where my brother and sisters went, started the year in January with the presentation of New Year gifts for good attendance and behaviour, in the year before. Each year we moved up a class until we left at the age of 12 or 13. It was a go-ahead school with a library and each week we could exchange a book during the afternoon. Books by Silas Hocking and Annie Swan were in great demand, so was Charles Dickens. School started at 9.30. After prayers our teacher would read a passage from the Bible and Moody and Sankey hymns were sung with gusto.

At 10.15 we went up some steps into the Chapel for prayers, reading of the lesson and a hymn. The choir included Mr. Wibberley, playing a fiddle, and sharing a music stand with Mr. Bradford, shoemaker, another fiddler. Mr. Smith a potter played a flute, Mr. Heafield, boot-and-shoe shop owner, sang tenor and Mr. David Tebbit, colliery weighing machine clerk, bass, Miss Buckley and Mrs. Smith were the ladies in the choir. There was no piano or organ to help.[21]

The children of Richard and Maria Hull were part of the first generation to take advantage of the Balfour Act: this had made secondary education available to all who had passed a test taken at the age of ten. Where classes in the Boys' department of the Council School each contained forty or more pupils, discipline was enforced with the use of a cane. Boys and girls who passed the Derbyshire Minor Scholarship Examination had the choice of going on to a grammar school at either Ashby or Burton. In 1921 Richard Albert Hull went to Ashby, followed the next year by his sister Kathleen. Parents who, unlike the Hulls, paid fees had to find £11 annually for the Girls' School or 12 guineas for the Boys'Grammar School. R.A. Hull, exceptionally good at both Maths and Physics, proceeded to St. John's College, Oxford and, after the war, was elected Fellow of Brasenose College. Tragically, in August 1949, Dr Hull met an early death at the age of 38, climbing the Brouillard Ridge of Mont Blanc in northern Italy.

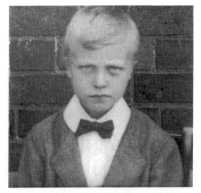

Richard Albert Hull aged 11

Comparable to his academic achievement was that of Geoffrey Arthur from Woodville, who went with a Classics Scholarship from Ashby to Oxford and from there after the war into the Foreign Office. There followed an ambassadorship, a knighthood and election to be Master of Pembroke College, Oxford.

The reverse side of such stories of success was undoubted lack of enthusiasm in many families at the emphasis on later achievements by pupils who had passed the 10 plus examination. A local historian, reporting from Castle Gresley, has commented on the 'creaming off' by neighbouring grammar schools of the cleverest children.[22] However, an intermediate-type Central School, serving the two Gresleys, had operated in Castle Gresley during the Depression and recovery years of the 1930s and into the war. It had language and science facilities, a flourishing laboratory and its own playing field. When the author left York Road Council School in 1929, it was only a few months after the opening of the Castle Gresley school.

SCHOOL REPORT, YORK ROAD COUNCIL SCHOOL 1921

FORM E. 13A.

Derbyshire Education Committee.

York Rd., Council School, Boys' Dept.

REPORT for term ending March 24th, 1921

Name of Scholar Albert Hull Age 9½

Class 1 No. in Class 41 Average Age 12¼

Position in Class 3rd

Attendance Absent no times

Punctuality No. of times late = 0

Conduct Satisfactory

Progress Satisfactory

Arithmetic	Mathematics	20	20
Composition	English	30	29
Handwriting	Recitation	10	9
Reading	Reading	10	9
Spelling	History	20	19
Drawing	Geography	20	18
Needlework	Drawing	20	12
Remarks	Handwork	10	7

Albert is conscientious + painstaking in his work + has made excellent progress

Signed W. B. White

147

1 VCH Derbys. Vol. II, p. 245.
2 Brit. Libr. Add. Mss. 6674 fol. 66. Will written at West Ham 17 Oct. 1683.
3 VCH. Derbys. Vol. II., p. 245.
4 Hillier, op. cit., p. 4.
5 Ibid., II, p. 28.
6 Hammond, J.L. & Barbara, The Town Labourer, 1760-1832, Longmans, 1978, p. 38.
7 Philip Heath, Melbourne, a tour of the town, (a brochure).
8 Hammond, JL & Barbara op. cit. p36
9 Hammond, op. cit., p. 38.
10 Collier, op. cit., p. 14.
11 Green, op. cit., p. 5.
12 Ibid., p. 9.
13 Parliamentary Papers, 1867, "Employment of Children, Young Persons and Women", p. 426.
14 Ibid., p. 428.
15 Parliamentary Papers, Royal Commission on Employment of Children, Young Persons and Women in Agriculture, 1867, Vol. 11.
16 M. Hull, m.s.
17 Collier, op. cit., p. 15: Derby Mercury ('situations vacant').
18 Derby Mercury, February 18 1863.
19 Hillier, op. cit.
20 Burton Chronicle, Jan. 23, 1893.
21 Maria Hull. m.s.
22 Beryl Greening, A Short History of 'The Streets in Castle Gresley, Derbyshire, 1996.

CHAPTER 11

CHANGE IN FARMING

Swings of prosperity and depression that characterised British farming during the Revolutionary and Napoleonic periods were surveyed by a former Member of Parliament for Derbyshire (Southern Division) in 1803. Sir George Crewe was concerned with the well-being of farming, and more than many other Members with the interests of the poorest constituents and he spoke of the war years with some feeling:

> "Farmers made money plentifully, paid high rents, spent money liberally, and employed all hands which the drafts for the Army and Navy had left behind. Did anyone complain of the Poor Rates then? Unquestionably not...
>
> But when the war ceased; when the tide of population swelled over the whole surface of the Kingdom ... when commerce opened her portals far and wide; when competition reduced the value of trade, and foreign produce crept in to vie with home manufactures; when the causes which had given an artificial and temporary value to land ceased – what happened then?
>
> Did the owners of land and tithes, taking into their prudent consideration the alteration of times and circumstances, prepare to retrace their stops and reduce rents and claims to meet present conditions? Alas! no...
>
> For a while, grumbling did nothing; the occupying farmer (who had, as farmers always do, when he got money, spent it liberally) began to pinch and scrape; bankruptcies became frequent; in the parish to which I before alluded, more than one half of the principal farmers, and the principal shop-keepers, came to beggary in a year or two."[1]

THE IMPLEMENTATION AND EFFECTS OF ENCLOSURE

When summarised, the procedure for implementing enclosure seems straightforward enough: a petition to Parliament to present a Bill, the granting of a Bill and the appointment of commissioners. The problem arose with the safeguarding of rights of those who might see themselves as likely to be disadvantaged. There would be those who saw themselves as almost certain to gain from the re-organisation of production: these were the wealthier members of the community. It was clear from the start that anyone wishing to be allocated land would need to pay his share of the cost of the reorganisation and consolidation that enclosure involved. Chambers finds that the 'true small farmer' with 30 or 40 acres, would have had reason for optimism when the petition was presented:

'... unless the enclosure was unusually costly, he would not have to find more than about £50 to £100, with the payments spread over a period of time. If we suppose that his land was reasonably fertile and that much of it had been open before the enclosure, then its value would probably have at least doubled in the enclosed state, and would have a market value of £23 or £30 per acre, in total say £900 for the whole farm. It follows that for an expenditure of £50 to £100 on enclosure his land increased in value from about £450 to £900.'[2]

Farey was full of enthusiasm: 'There cannot remain a doubt, but Inclosures have been and continue to be highly beneficial, in every point of view'.[3] There have been much less enthusiastic observers. As Pauline Gregg points out,[4] it was not until 1774 that it became necessary to give written notice (posted on the church door of the parish concerned) of the proposed petition. If the owner of the strips in the common field could not find the necessary capital (she suggests a £200 minimum for the average freeholder) he

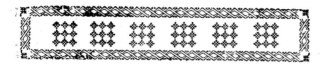

AN

A   C   T

FOR

Dividing and Inclofing the Common and Open Fields, Meadows, Paftures, and Common or Moor, within the Liberties of *Marſton upon Dove*, *Hatton*, *Hoon*, and *Hoon Hay*, in the Pariſh of *Marſton upon Dove*, in the County of *Derby*.

ꟽꟽꟽꟽꟽ Ⱨ Ⱨ Ⱨ Ⱨ Ⱨ **ꟲ Ⰳ Ⱃ Ⰵ ꝛ Ꝛ Ꞅ** there are within the Pariſh of *Marſton* **Preamble.**
    upon Dove, in the County of *Derby*, and the Liberty
of *Hatton* in the fame Pariſh, feveral Common and
Open Fields, Meadows, and Paftures, containing together Four hundred and Eighty Acres, or thereabouts, and there is a certain Common or Moor,
called *Hatton Moor*, Part lying in the Manor or Lordſhip of *Hatton*
aforefaid, and the Remainder within the Hamlets or Liberties of
Marſton upon Dove and *Hoon*, within the faid Pariſh of *Marſton
upon Dove* aforefaid, containing Three hundred and Fifty Acres,
or thereabouts:

And whereas the KING's Moft Excellent MAJESTY, in Right
of his Duchy of *Lancaſter*, is Lord of the Manor of *Hatton*, and
the Right honourable *George Venables* Lord *Vernon* is the Leffee
of the faid Manor of *Hatton* for a Term of Years now fubfifting,
and as fuch claims the Right of Soil of and in fuch Part of the
faid Common or Moor called *Hatton Moor* as lies within the faid
Manor of *Hatton*:

A

And

Opening page of the 1789 Enclosure Act
for Marston upon Dove and area

A farm in Stapenhill, 1824. Painted by P. Harrington

would have to sell his allotment and find that he had to pay for the sale.

Legal owners of common rights were compensated for the loss of them, following enclosure, with an allocation of land, but this was very likely to be too small to be economic, to be less than the three acre limit that was generally accepted as necessary to sustain a cow. This was the situation for those who owned their houses threatened by re-allocation: if they were only tenants they had no right to compensation. Labourers wishing to protest against an enclosure proposal had to submit their claim in writing – an often impossible task for those who were likely to be illiterate.[5]

Very often, enclosure would produce enrichment and impoverishment at the same time. In the north of the region, the process left most of the land occupied by very large or substantial holdings. At Chellaston, its '890 acres of good corn land'[6] were divided after enclosure in 1804 between twenty proprietors: Sir George Crewe had 300 acres; Henry Orton 80 and George Wotton 60 acres. The perpetual curate of the parish had been allotted 54 acres in lieu of tithes.

The Victoria County History of Derbyshire shows only 45,028 acres in the county as having been enclosed before 1802 with another 46,675 acres enclosed between 1802 and 1845.[7] But, as Chambers has recorded, most enclosure in the early part of the 18th century had been not by Act, but by agreement.[8] During the reign of George I (1714-27)[9] only eighteen Acts of Enclosure were passed for land in Derbyshire but by the end of the 18th century a total of 2,500 such Acts had been passed for the county.

ENCLOSURE IN SOUTH DERBYSHIRE

Parish	Date of Act	Acreage enclosed
Aston-on-Trent	1763	1500
Chellaston	1804	700
Egginton	1791	980
Etwall	1797	834
Hartshorne	1766	917
Melbourne	1787	
Ockbrook	1772	700
Ravenstone	1760	750
Repton	1766	636
Smisby	1826	550
Spondon	1788	471
Stapenhill		100
Ticknall	1765	
Willington	1768	1300

As with other such measures, the Hartshorne enclosure[10] of

1765 was based upon principles of proportionality: a landowner's holdings that had previously been distributed over scattered strips of the open fields, were to be consolidated into compact areas of the same approximate total size. Included in land to be redistributed was the product of previous enclosures that might go back to Tudor times. Concerning land that came up for redistribution, it was provided under the Act, that redistribution could involve the exchange of parcels of land, providing that this transfer was done by 29 September 1766.

Enclosures were intended to enhance business efficiency, there was another essential principle: the existing social order should not be disturbed, so that the squire and his relations, the parson and the local gentry would all retain their place in society. In Hartshorne, the Rev. William Cant, Lord of the Manor, was given property equal to his previous acreage. Likewise, the Rector, the Rev. William Astley, as befitted a trustee of the Church, was allocated land equal in

Findern Smithy c. 1916 – horse power remained essential to farming well into the 20th century

value and quality to the existing glebe[11] and sheep pasture and was given further acreage to compensate for loss of tithes he had previously received. There were allocated to him lands of equivalent value. Thus the Rev. Astley was allocated in compensation a total of 336 acres – replacing the cost of lost tithes. The Rector received in addition 43 acres in compensation for the loss of the glebe lands.

Most of the rearranged land that came to the Rector after enclosure was taken out of the Great Common – it was sold in 1922, when with 168 acres it was advertised as a 'capital mixed dairy farm', noted for the quality of its cheese.

A major beneficiary under the Enclosure, John Taylor, was allocated with his family 64 acres to add to the 105 acres in their possession before Enclosure. A part of Mr. Taylor's allocation had resulted from an exchange with the Earl of Chesterfield, whose seat was at Bretby.[12]

The most serious and long term effect of enclosure was upon the poorest land users, who had shared access in a truly communal element of living.

Farey described what he had been told of one local incident:[13]

"The history which I heard, of the Inclosure of Ashby Wolds: (near, and indeed within the Circuit of this County, tho' in Leicestershire), appeared to me very extraordinary. In the beginning of the first Year of the Commissioners' acting, they declared the extinction of the Common Rights, and after driving off the Cattle, the Wolds lay entirely unoccupied, while the public Roads were fencing off, and during the next two Years, the Commissioners let the large Fields thus formed, to be either grazed or ploughed, at the option of the Tenants: and 200 Acres were ploughed, and cropped a second time with Oats, and the whole produce carried off, by these temporary Tenants, before the Allotments were made."

At Chaddesden, east of Derby and north of the Derwent, 211 acres of Common land were among the 900 acres enclosed by the Act of 31 George III. In the village of 500 people, with a total acreage of 2089 acres, 1607 of them belonging to Sir Robert Wilmot, who according to Speed[14] was of Saxon descent. In Stuart times, a Wilmot married Dorothy, daughter of Sir George Gresley of Drakelow.

Commons and waste continued to be greatly significant to small holders, such as William Payne of Church Gresley, living in mid-19th century on the edge of Gresley Common. The scene there was described by his son Joseph:

"My father had two fields with the house, and during the summer months he used to turn two or three beasts and a pony or two on the Common and shut the fields up for mowing. We used to rear a flock of geese. Every year we had 40 or 50 geese grazing on the Common. In my early days it was surprising the amount of keep which the horses that were turned on got. There would be anywhere from a dozen to 15 or more horses, and sometimes a donkey or 2 there."

Joseph Payne.[15]

There were many legal problems arising from the attempts of those with Common rights physically to protect their access by erecting fences and often huts. The supervision of rights passed to urban district councils in 1894. It had been easy for the law to evict squatters from Common land in the early days of enclosure, but now householders were claiming that they sought to protect the Common from further encroachment and loss. Swadlincote Urban District Council met in 1905 to discuss such a case:

"...in accordance with instructions, a portion of the fence erected on the Common by Mrs. Illsley had been taken down by the surveyor, and five panes of glass in a window of the house had been broken." M. Hull ms

A supplementary report stated that a writ had been issued on the Council by Mrs. Illsley's solicitor, seeking to restrain the Council from further interfering with her property. The clerk was authorised to take the necessary steps to defend the Council's position.

Mr. Howard suggested that it would be more dignified for the Council to proceed against some strong corporation defaulter, before they went on with the case against Mrs. Illsley. The report was approved.[16]

FARMING IN THE 1860s

There was a marked pastoral emphasis to the 1867 parliamentary survey of South Derbyshire farming.[17] Its area extended northwards from Repton across the wide flood-plain of the Trent and Dove. The overall impression is of small tenant farms. A few were run by the farmer's family alone, with help needed only at harvest time.

A dependence in this northern part of South Derbyshire on milk production was likely to require some labour to live on the farm. The alternative was seen at Hilton, with a cow-man needing to walk two miles from his cottage in order to start milking at 5 a.m. There was a marked division of labour, with women tending to be allocated the uncomplicated tasks of weeding ploughland and picking stones to which at Hilton were added hoeing corn and hay-making. An informative farmer at Scropton supplied more detail, with "two or three [women] in summer weeding and haymaking; some work by the piece (by the thrave) shearing in harvest time, [for which] I pay them 1s a day"; adding that, for the male workers concerned, "if it was not for the beer, the winter work supplied by the Burton breweries would be a blessing to our labourers."

Extras were of great value to the farm labourers: the pig

"Some of the cottages are good . . . " rural cottages in Clifton Road,
Netherseal 1904

By courtesy of C. Liversuch

'or two' kept by many of them, but the 1867 survey
recorded widespread regret among agricultural labourers
and their families that the old practice of allowing farm
workers to keep cows "... in the lanes" – three or four at a
time, at Repton and Egginton, particularly in summer had
been discontinued at the behest of the farmers.

Generally, it was a hard life, with much less than £1 per
week available for a family containing five, six or more
children, and parents would often make a sacrifice, enabling
children to obtain some grounding in a school. Added to
which, some of the cottages were said in the survey to have
been in a deplorable condition: in Church Broughton, "some
of the cottages are good, some moderate, some scarcely fit
for habitation. Some of them are very inconveniently
situated with respect to the farms...... some of them are
small and close."[18]

South Derbyshire: labour data from sample farms (1867)

Parish	Population	Acreage	Wages (men) Weekly s.d. winter/summer	Wages (men) Yearly (living in) £	Hours of work Men	Hours of work Boys	Hours of work Women	Starting age Boys	Starting age Girls	Distance from work
Barton Blount	73	1,150	n/a[1]				8am-5pm	n/a		0.5miles
Church Broughton	651	2,272	14/- 16/-		5am-6pm	6am-6pm		13	13	1.5 miles
Eggington	355	2,289	13/- 10/-[2]	£8 - £14	6.30am-5.30pm	8am-5pm		10[3]	10	
Elvaston	500	2,500	14/-		6am-6pm			12		
Hilton	719	1,120	14/- 16/-	£12 - £15[4]	5am start			10/11		2 miles
Repton (without Bretby)	1843 (384)		12/- 14/- to 16/-	£12 - £16[5]				12		
Scropton[6]	819	5,054	13/- 14/-					16[7]		

Notes
1. Not available: wages for boy waggoner, young boy bird tenderer, women on harvest work
2. Plus "fool's beer"
3. Exceptionally from eight years old
4. 15 year old lad, £2 per annum
5. 12 year old lads, £4 per annum
6. At Scropton some married women work four months harvesting, earning 1/- to 2/6 per day. Elsewhere, women's wages were not given
7. Team drivers are younger
8. Hazlewood and Shottle (Belper Union), men earned 9/6 per acre hoeing beans, and 5/6 per acre hoeing wheat or £13 yearly living in, plus food

Source: Parliamentary Papers, Commission on Agriculture - Employment of Children, Young People and Women, 1867

159

Near to the Trent, farming was very dependent on grazing, whilst beyond Derby, arable farming became more important.

HAZELWOOD AND SHOTTLE
Population, 819 – Acreage, 5,054

The Rev. J. Jenkins reported to the Commission:

"Our cottages are very bad, there is rarely more than one bedroom in them, in which adults and children crowd together. This is partly owing to the circumstance that they belong to small proprietors, who are desirous to get as much as possible at the least outlay. The farms in Hazelwood are small, the tenant farmers poor, consequently they avoid as much as possible giving employment to labourers. In winter many are out of work, and they look to harvest as the time of compensation.

28a. Evidence of Mr. Jos. Goodwin, farmer: – "Labour can sometimes hardly be got for money in this neighbourhood; this year a man asked me 9s an acre for hoeing beans, and I have had to pay 7s 6d. When we can get hands we pay about 5s 6d an acre for hoeing wheat. I have 140 acres, of which 40 acres are arable; I only keep one man besides my son, and he's not a full man; he has 13l and his keep, a full man would have 18l. We have no cottage attached to the farm." (These farm buildings are in a wretched state. The farm belongs to the trustees of some charity, and nothing is ever done by the landowners to improve the state of affairs –G.C.)[19]

Mr. G. Culley was co-ordinator of the survey for Derbyshire.

Mr. T.S. Farmer had nearly three miles to travel from his house to the osier beds of the Dove plain, with its meanders and ox-bow lakes:

Cattle graze in Barehills Vale, Melbourne

"I have osier beds on the banks of the Dove, at Etwall and Egginton; the peeling season is from the end of April to the beginning or middle of June; in the peeling season I employ all the hands I can get, women and children, mothers bring their babies in cradles with them, whole families work together, the mother breaks the peel (draws the willow through a break), and the children peel. They do it by the bundle, some families will earn 4s or 5s a week. One woman I employ can peel about two bundles a day, at 6d a bundle (size of bundle, 38 inches). The women I employ in light farm work I pay 5s a week, 6s a week in harvest. In this parish I could get as many women (married) as I like, in the next parish (Egginton) few women work out, they have no public-house at Egginton, and the families are better off."[20]

SOUTH DERBYSHIRE FARMING CONDITIONS (SUMMARY)

SOUTH DERBYSHIRE
23. Mr John Shaw, landsurveyor, freeholder, and occupier, says, "South Derbyshire is in great part a pastoral district."

"Boys are to a limited extent employed from 10 to 11 years of age in light work during spring and summer, and as plough boys or farm servants from about 13 or 14."

"Girls are only employed as household servants excepting sometimes in harvest; they go out to service early."

"The mode of living, rate of wages and earnings, vary very much in different localities. In the neighbouhood of large towns and populous mining districts the wages of an agricultural labourer will be 15s a week, with 'bargain' work in summer, when 18s to 21s will be earned. In some of the outlying districts a low rate of wages prevails from 11s to 13s a week, with extras in summer, but generally in the purely agricultural districts 13s or 14s are the average rate of wages, with extra work and increased earnings in the summer. In the first case the weekly earnings of a labourer and his wife and family will average 17s to 18s a week, in the second case about 13s, and in the latter the average will be 15s or 16s a week. In the populous districts and near a town rents are from 2s to 3s a week, and in other districts 1s 2d to 1s 10d per week."

"The mode of living is generally bread and potatoes, with bacon and cheese, and I believe most families now manage to have a fair supply of butcher's meat." [21]

Dalton's table of land use in South Derbyshire in 1870[22] shows much more concentration on permanent grass north of the Trent than south of it. Over the 70 year period of Dalton's study, barley had increased in significance and oats greatly diminished.

Enclosure by combining scattered holdings in the northern part of the region had accelerated the advantage to grass imported from sites enjoying the favourable soil and relief conditions that did not exist in the Keuper marls and sandstones of the south. Farmers had to adjust to difficult economic times: the jump in corn prices in wartime after

Grazing land on the Trent flood plain seen here from Wllington Power
Station in 1957

1800; the peacetime market slide that lasted until the middle of the century.[23] Any such movements disadvantaged grain as against milk producers.

Most Derbyshire enclosures had taken place in the 18th Century: Etwall's 834 acres were enclosed by an Act dated 1797; but Smisby, then in Derbyshire, had its 550 acres enclosed by George IV, in 1826, at a time when corn prices were slipping. Parliament, in Napoleonic war fever, had investigated the factors affecting food supply, especially for the poor. Enquiry was made into the effect of enclosure on wheat acreage, with investigators having to rely on returns at a parish level made by officiating clergy.[24]

Etwall's area under wheat decreased by 85 acres during the short period 1797-1801. But at Repton where enclosure dated from 1776, and the soil was lighter than Etwall's, land under wheat had increased by 20 acres.

Whilst the wide flood plain of the middle Trent was particularly suitable – apart from flood risk – for permanent grazing, it had long been known that over-use could lead to deterioration that required manuring to help rectify.[25] Where phosphates had become depleted by over-cropping or weathering, the traditional method had been to dress the land with application of bones.[26] The Lords Committee introduced a further factor – the choice of cattle breed. Beasts bought and introduced from 'the north' had not done so well on either side of the middle Trent.[27]

In the mid-19th century, cattle farmers benefited from the availability for feed of brewers' grains from Burton, whilst railways began to be useful to many parts of the farm economy, including the movement to market of stock and farm products. Cheese production before 1870 increased using surplus milk and quality improved.[28]

1   Crewe, Sir George, <u>A Word for the Poor</u>, Address to both Houses of Parliament 1803.
2   Chambers, Jonathan David & Mingay, Gordon Edmund,

The Agricultural revolution, 1750-1880, B.T. Batsford: London, 1966, p. 89.
3   Farey, op. cit., Vol II, p. 77.
4   Gregg, op.cit., pp. 28-9.
5   Chambers & Mingay, op. cit. p. 99; Gregg, op. cit., p. 29.
6   Glover. op. cit. Vol. II. p. 254.
7   VCH Derbys. Vol. II.
8   Chambers & Mingay, op. cit. p. 82.
9   VCH ibid.
10 Spavold, Janet, At the sign of the Bulls Head: a history of Hartshorne and its enclosure, South Derbyshire Local History Research Group: Woodville, c. 1985.
11 Ibid., p. 68. Glebe was land allocated to contribute to a church's income.
12 Ibid., p. 86.
13 Farey, op. cit. Vol. 2, p. 29.
14 Glover, op. cit. p. 205.
15 Letter to Burton Mail.
16 Burton Observer, 14th September 1905.
17 Parliamentary Papers, 1867, "Employment of Children, Young Persons and Women in Agriculture", 1869, p. 428.
18 Ibid., 1869, p. 426.
19 Ibid., 1867, p. 425.
20 Ibid., Evidence to Select Committee, p. 427.
21 Parliamentary Papers, Agriculture (1867) Select Committee, pp. 426-7.
22 Dalton, R.J., Agricultural Change in South Derbyshire 1800-1870, East Midland Geographer Vol. 20, 1997, p. 38.
23 Robert Allen, Agriculture during The Industrial Revolution: Economic History of Britain since 1700. Vol. 1, p. 97.
24 Select Committee on Agric., evidence by William Smith, 8 July 1833.
25 Dalton, op. cit. p. 38, quoting Carrington, W.T., "Our Dairy Farming", Journ. Royal Agric Soc. of England, Second Series, 1865, p. 344.
26 Dalton, ibid.
27 House of Lords Select Committee on Agriculture, 8 June 1833.
28 Dalton, op. cit., p. 74.

CHAPTER 12

INDUSTRY IN SOUTH DERBYSHIRE

ECONOMIC TRENDS

The 19th century saw a remarkable advance in production from the South Derbyshire coalfield, where there was a happy coincidence of coal and clay and great numbers of labourers were required for their extraction. The coal was dug from ever lower levels. Yellow clay found with the shallow coal produced a rapidly growing earthenware industry, so that what started as a village settlement could rapidly become part of an urban area. The pottery industry that had begun with local materials needed before long to bring in kaolin (china clay) to manufacture some items of kitchen ware. The need for economical transport was met by South Derbyshire's central position where first the canals and then rail links became available for bulk freight movement.

Collieries multiplied after 1800 and mineral or 'tram' lines were laid down to carry coal from pit to canal or rail and then to further markets. The collier and the potter replaced the farm labourer on census returns, though farming remained the lead occupation in the Trent valley between Burton and Shardlow. During the 19th century graphs show striking differences between Weston-upon-Trent, Melbourne and the coalfield townships.

In order to understand the willingness of a rural labour force to work in the unhealthy, often dangerous environment of the mines and factories it is necessary to look at the realities of life on the land in the early 19th century.

Labourers' weekly wages on Derbyshire farms during the 18th century had hovered about or just above subsistence level, starting at 7s and increasing to about 8s at the beginning of the Napoleonic Wars. Competition for labour –

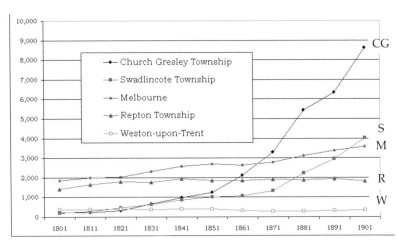

source: Victoria County History (Derbyshire) Vol 2

for instance from the canal that passed Shardlow's door, could bring wages up to between 10s and 12s, but this was still short of the 14s maximum obtainable by labour on farms enclosed in neighbouring Nottinghamshire's Sherwood Forest region.[2]

Much of social ferment in the countryside during and after the period of war with the French was related to drastic changes that had occurred in land tenure, with many farmers having lost possession of their holdings. Labourers had found sudden changes to the price of basic foods that drove them to conditions of desperate poverty. Farey said there were few workers on the land at the turn of century who could manage on what their labour could earn. There were identifiable seasonal rhythms to income: work was plentiful at harvest-time when farmers were calling out for help and day labourers could expect at least the equivalent of 12s and sometimes much more per week; but in idle winter months, they would be sent round to employers of the parish in search of work. They would then be 'doing the

POPULATION TRENDS IN SOUTH DERBYSHIRE 1801-1901[1]

	1801	1811	1821	1831	1841	1851	1861	1871	1881	1891	1901
1. Church Gresley parish	1180	1635	1951	2543	2796	3300	4416	6243	10259	12654	16458
Church Gresley Township	245	235	306	671	993 1	257	2108	3297	5422	6317	8627
Swadlincote Township	216	296	459	645	858	1007	1076	1343	2214	2945	4017
2. Melbourne	1861	2003	2027	2301	2583	2680	2622	2781	3123	3369	3580
3. Repton	1689	1989	2104	2083	2241	2232	2177	2248	2205	2293	2158
Repton Township	1424	1648	1802	1758	1943*	1863	1853	1902	1869	1926	1807
Bretby Chapel	265	341	302	325	298	369	324	346	336	367	351
4. Weston-upon-Trent	380	362	397	387	396	399	321	294	292	322	353

*Repton Township – a considerable number of persons temporarily present in 1841 owing to the village wake.

168

rounds' and would for that reason be called roundsmen. The situation of tenant farmers in the Trent Valley was addressed in Parliamentary Select Committee hearings of July, 1833. Evidence from a land agent to Sir George Crewe and Sir Henry Harpur, two of the largest landowners in the region, gave a picture of improved farm practices, with substantial reduction in tenants' rents but some tenant farmers were 'very much oppressed even upon those rents'.

Parliament, in considering the impact of enclosure, was concerned at the likely effect of prices upon poor rates. In South Derbyshire local prices for corn were lower than the national average, but showed a similar rising trend.

WHOLESALE WHEAT PRICES
(in shillings per quarter)

Derby [3]			National Averages[4]
April 1807	54	1807	73/-
Sept. 1807	52		
April 1808	56	1808	78/-
Sept. 1808	73		
April 1809	68	1809	94/-
Sept. 1809	87		

The Lords, in committee, were in effect looking for evidence to justify decisions that had already been taken, if not recorded. Their deliberations had taken place in a situation of increasing seriousness. The Select Committee's brief was to devise a "means of remedying in some degree the existing evil of adding to the wages of labour from the poor rate."[4]

They sought reluctantly a strategy for intervention, whilst alleging that the destitute were to some degree responsible for their poverty. The legislators claimed to be seeking a "mode of finding employment for those who profess themselves unable to abstain it".[5] Their lordships' view of starving families suggested that they meant both to punish the poor for past misdeeds and to deter them from being unable to provide for themselves in the future. They insisted that there had been abuses in procedures for relief that had become an ever-growing burden for communities. The Lords proposed measures that were to be always within the ability of local officers to execute. So the Government was moving towards work provision, under conditions: "that the parish should, if possible, provide them (the unemployed) with labour less acceptable in its nature, than ordinary labour and at lower rates than the average rate of the Neighbourhood."[6] In such an unsympathetic climate people had little choice but to take whatever work was available, moving off the land into unpleasant, often dangerous industrial jobs.

SOCIETY AND STATUS

Meanwhile, for the ruling classes there had been little change to their social status. Burdett's map of 1791 identified South Derbyshire's country seats and their occupants. By 1821, a Harpur had left Calke Abbey to his son, the redoubtable Sir George Crewe, whilst Bretby Hall stayed with the Earls of Chesterfield and Drakelow with the Gresleys. Only an extension of the franchise in the Reform Bill of 1832 began to disturb a society traditionally led by local notables.[7]

NOBILITY AND LANDED GENTRY

Abney Edward Esq., Measham Hall
Brown Sir Wm. Cave, Stretton-in-the-fields
Burdett Sir Francis, Foremark Hall
Chesterfield the Earl of, Bretby Hall
Crewe Sir George, Calke Abbey
Farnham the Countess of, Catton Hall
Gresley Sir Roger, Drakelow
Hastings Sir Charles, Willesley
Lamb the Hon. George, Melbourne Hall

Calke Abbey: South West view. c.1829

SAND, CLAY AND COAL

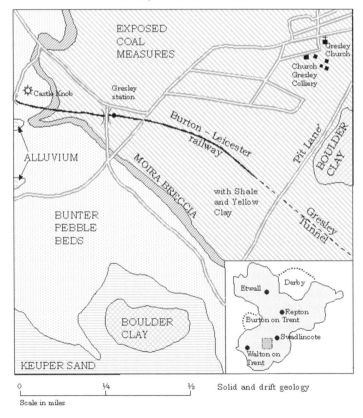

EXPOSED
COAL
MEASURES

Gresley
Church

Church
Gresley
Colliery

Castle Knob

Gresley
station

Burton – Leicester
railway

Pit Lane

BOULDER
CLAY

ALLUVIUM

MOIRA BRECCIA

with Shale
and Yellow
Clay

Gresley
Tunnel

BUNTER
PEBBLE
BEDS

BOULDER
CLAY

KEUPER SAND

Etwall

Derby

Burton on Trent

Repton

Swadlincote

Walton on
Trent

0   ¼   ½   Solid and drift geology

Scale in miles

171

COAL

The Coal Measures of the South Derbyshire coalfield lie to the west, and those of the Leicestershire field to the east of the Ashby anticline. Deep mining in South Derbyshire was always inhibited, geologically, as a result of earth movement and contortions that produced faults with a maximum downthrow (the Linton fault) of 2,200 feet.[8] But these disadvantages were balanced by the thickness of seams and the multiplicity of outcrops – the first such coal to be accessible at Swadlincote belonging to the Dicky Gobbler seam. Between Swadlincote and Newhall, the Main coal approached the surface seam with impressive dimensions of 10-16 feet thickness. The first large-scale colliery in the district, Donisthorpe, at a point on the Leicestershire border, was sunk to the Main coal.

EARLY MINES

Only the relatively wealthy, in mediaeval times, could afford the luxury of coal fires. Large-scale demand existed in London, but there was no viable route there for coal from the East Midlands (except for one or two precious sites near the tidal portion of the Trent). Nonetheless coal was mined in South Derbyshire in the mediaeval period. As long ago as 1293, an ordinary charter of conveyance from Henry de Verdun to Thomas of Alrewas left Henry the profit from 'sea-coals and other minerals' found in Swadlincote land[9]... the vaguer reference to the Blackepit in 1208 has already been noted. In 1481 there is a reference to the same area which is much more precise: 'half an acre of land ... lying in Blackhyll in the fields of Swadlincote, in which half acre of land there are now coal mines'.[10] In 1562 coal mines in Swadlincote were alienated to Christopher Alleyn. When Alleyn was indicted for High Treason reference was made merely to, 'the selling and letting over of the cole Pytte of Swadlincote, with the profit thereof'.[11] There is a much more substantial record, dated five years later, to Swadlincote coals and the involvement of the Dethick family of Newhall.[12]

1567 GRANT OF COAL MINING RIGHTS IN SWADLINCOTE BY FYNDERNE TO DETHICK:[13]

...between Thos. F. late of Nuneaton in the county of Warwick ... and Humfey Dethick of Newhall ... and Elizabeth, his wife,... the said T.F. for and upon the consid. of the sum of ten pounds ... doth demise and let to farm to the said H. and E. and their assigns, all that or those the mine or mines, pit and pits, of coals of the said Thomas being within the town and fields of Swad ... with frank and free entry, ingress, egress and free access and passage with cart and carriage to and from the said mines ... and free employees to dig and get the coals of the said mines ... and free liberty as well to dig and sink new pits and essay to find new mines of coal in all and singular the said lands ... and of all the coals ... to take and convert to the proper uses of the said H. and E.; as also to occupy and dig in, by and throughout all the old mines there, if any such there be, to have, hold ... for the term of their two lives ... yielding and paying for the premises unto the said Thomas Fynderne and his heirs one load of coals for and by every year in which H. and E. or their assigns ... shall dig and get coal...

Witn: Roger Churt, William Gifford, William Dixe, John Morley and others, 10 March 9 Eliz. (1567).

There is also reference in Elizabeth I's reign to the sale of two mines in Swadlincote and Oakthorpe for £20.[14] During the Commonwealth a Puritan's petition demanded action against the rector of Seale for 'conniving with colliers in an ale-house every Saturday night'.[15]

In the 18th century, the market for coal increased

dramatically due to the demand for fuel to drive forward the industrial revolution. With the development of techniques for raising and utilising steam to heat boilers, drive machinery and smelt iron, the fortunes of Midland coal owners were transformed. Every extra demand for furnace and boiler fuel created a greater impetus for speedier delivery of coal at a reasonable price – processes played out in the canal and railway-building eras. Then the situation was further changed at the end of the 19th century with the building of power stations in the Trent valley. These looked to coal to feed them and of course the fuel was carried on coal-burning trains, each of them with a locomotive engineer (driver) and fireman.

Mawe in his 'Minerals of Derbyshire' (1802) showed on his small-scale map only three collieries in South Derbyshire, all of them within a radius of a mile from Newhall as against the seven pits, accompanied by the 'fire engine', a coal-fired steam pumping engine shown at Measham on Prior's plan[16]

Bretby No. 3 ('Stanton Lane') Colliery, 1872-1962
© Courtesy of Magic Attic Archives

174

of 1775-7. The leading economic historian writing at the time, John Farey, gives the pits operating in 1810: Blackfordby, Littleworth, Milk Hill, Gosley Waste (Hartshorne) Measham, Oakthorpe, Donisthorpe, Bretby, Hallfields, Newhall, Newhall Park, Stanton, Swadlincote, Wooden Box, Waterfield, Woodfield and Warren Hill Furnace.[17] By 1831, driven on by the prospect of great profits and with the advantage of new machinery and techniques for shaft sinking ten collieries had gone down to the Main coal.

1800	Donisthorpe (Old Colliery)	1821	Rawdon
1804	Moira Double Pit	1825	Granville No.1
1806	Furnace Pit	1829	Church Gresley
1812	Donisthorpe	1830	Hastings and Grey
1813	Bath Pit	1831	Stanton

There followed, geographically, an increase in the density of colliery distribution[18]

1853	Gresley Wood	1860	Cadley Hill
1854	Old White House	1860	Matts Yard
1854	Swadlincote	1871	Donisthorpe
1857	Oakthorpe (Canal Pit)	1871/5	Coton Park
1857	Netherseal	1874	Bretby
1857	Cartwrights	1887	Granville No.2

Wages on the coalfields were not high, but they were good enough to attract workers from the land to the mine. Hewers' wages were reckoned, reasonably, by weight, and were usually therefore given as an average. Labourers could sometimes be classed as casually employed. A hewer's daily average wage at Swadlincote in 1841 was 3s 4d per day, as compared with 3s 8d at Moira. Labourers had been earning 2s per day at Measham mines in 1791 whilst at Gresley, in 1834, they got only 2s 6d. Boys aged 12 to 16 at Shipley (on the main coalfield north of Derby) were taking home 1s 3d to 1s 6d.[19]

The employment of young boys was to become a matter of public concern. In 1842 Andrew Blake, M.D., stated of colliers in Derbyshire, that he had observed that many of them were 'not so tall as their neighbours in other employment'; this, in a degree, he considered, was 'owing to their being employed too young.'[20]

Given the particularly dangerous nature of mining, it was intolerable to liberal opinion that miners' pay and even more, their conditions should be so poor, but such sentiments belonged to a minority. Unrestrained free enterprise demanded that progress – the pursuit of higher productivity and profits – be pursued at all costs. It needed the force of campaigners inside and outside Parliament to provide some intervention at least on behalf of a minimum employment age. It had long been evident to workers themselves that they must combine to have any chance of reaching better bargains with their employers. There was a great controversy over the Combination Acts and it was due especially to the work of Francis Place that they were repealed in 1824 when it became legal again to resume union and, radicals hoped, political activity to further what had been gained by the Reform Act of 1832.

Miners in South Derbyshire came out on strike for higher pay in 1844. Nearly half a century later, in 1892-3 there was another, protracted strike at Granville Colliery, Church Gresley, which ended with a lock-out, failure and dismissal of strikers.

CHURCH GRESLEY COLLIERY

Church Gresley, lying upon the exposed Coal Measures, had many small pits in the late 18th century on the higher ground overlooking Castle Gresley. The most accessible seams had been reached by adit mining, where tubs could be pulled out at an incline by either man or beast (it was not

Church Gresley Colliery showing main coal screens and the old and new pits
1918

Church Gresley Colliery from the north 1918

Church Gresley Colliery No. 1 pit screens 1918

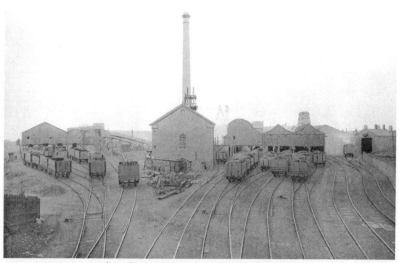

Church Gresley Colliery from the south
showing screen and No. 1 winding engine house 1918

until much later that ponies were taken down to underground workings). Where shafts had been sunk they were to relatively shallow depths compared to later engineering feats. Men were lowered down these shafts, two at a time, astride a rod in a basket-like container, to work two stalls. Only twelve men would be below ground at any one time, each of them working a 12-hour shift. Food cooked by their womenfolk would be taken to the pit and sent down to the workings.[21]

Gresley New Pit was sunk in 1834, replacing a shaft sunk by Gregory of Repton in 1829. The New Pit (hours of work

Mr P. Beaumont, manager of Church Gresley Colliery, appointed in 1897

12 hours a day, 6 days a week) was owned by the Marquis of Hastings, whose family had been connected for centuries with the coal-mining industry in Leicestershire. Another shaft to the same mine, the 'Upcast', was sunk in 1865. The Main coal was worked until the seam was deemed economically to have been exhausted, which meant in practice that seven feet of nether coal was left, when operations moved on. Eventually, with the easiest and most profitable coals having been taken out, it was decided to return and sink new shafts to the old workings, or redevelop old ones. The upcast shaft, which earlier had been sunk to the Little seam, was rebricked in 1897 and taken down successively to the Woodfield Stockings and Eureka seams. Finally the Kilburn was reached at 480 yards depth in March 1898.[22]

It was greatly to the advantage of the Moira Colliery Company (the owners of the Church Gresley Colliery from the mid 19th century) that they could move their output by rail along the Woodville Loop. Before its construction in 1883 coal had been shifted along a tramway to Cut End and the Ashby Canal. Coal companies built pit rows – large terraced complexes – for their workers and families. At Church Gresley such accommodation, with very basic amenities, was located on the south side of the square bordered on one side by the parish church and churchyard. A pillar of reinforcing coal support was left beneath the church – extremely valuable for the future, when subsidence, especially from the shallower seams, could be apprehended.

Much of the rapid growth of population on the South Derbyshire coalfield in the first half of the 19th century was due to inward migration from agricultural districts to north and south, but the statistics of Chandler[23] suggest that there was also a significant movement from Leicestershire north of the Ashby-Bardon Hill line – an area containing that county's older mines. There is a symmetry in the pattern of population growth / decline. The counties were connected on a good turnpike road, leading towards the Derbyshire pits by way of Boundary and Wooden Box (Woodville).

THE CLAY AND POTTERY INDUSTRIES

There was a pottery at Ticknall in the 16th century according to George Eckersley[24] and other small pottery concerns have since been found to have operated there at the time, making earthen vessels, pots and pancheons. Production at Ticknall had declined very much by the end of the 18th century owing, Pilkington said,[25] to enclosure, making it much more difficult for potters to obtain suitable clay. This was a reasonable assessment, given the problems developers had eventually in finding raw material that would perform well.

In 1790, James Woodward, using yellow clay found with the local coal deposits, started making bricks at Swadlincote

– some for local use and others (firebricks) intended for steel-works in Sheffield. In 1793 Moses Jones began the manufacture of pancheons, as had been done before at Ticknall. His pottery was to the west of the site of the first Granville Colliery and the kilns were fired with peat or coal dug in surface workings near Woodhouse Junction. At the same time, Hunt and Bourne were making firebricks in Swadlincote, at the rear of lower Coppice Side. There were many changes of ownership among the first-comers and in the 1840s James Woodward took over brick making from Hunt. Meanwhile the Ensor family, later one of the largest operators in the region, began to take an active interest in their business at the Pool firebrick works.

POTTERY FIRMS IN SWADLINCOTE – GRESLEY IN 1850

Sankey	Harrison & Shaw	Jones
Wileman	Mason Cash	Banks
Woodward	Cooper & Massey	Chapman & Hunt
Hough	Redfern	Sharpe

There was intermarriage among the leading families. Cooper's daughter married Nehemiah Banks, whose firm later merged with Mason Cash.

The vast demand for pipes that could be used to carry factory and domestic waste to sewage works promoted the rapid growth of South Derbyshire firms making salt-glazed pipes of all dimensions – the biggest weighing almost a ton. They also produced the bends, junctions, traps, and channels in the same material, and of enormous variety:[26] There were quoted 1400 types of junction alone. They also supplied the rapidly growing market for sanitary ware (especially water closets) demanded by the revolution in hygiene. In 1872, Thomas Wragg, bringing with him employees from Loxley, Sheffield, began the large-scale manufacture in Swadlincote of sanitary pipes of all dimensions. In the 1870s also,

The Stacking Yard, Woodwards Pipe Works, Swadlincote

Aerial view of John Knowles Pipe Works, Woodville

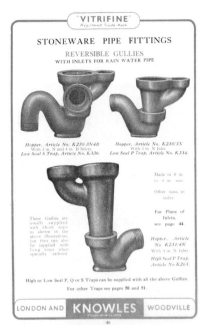

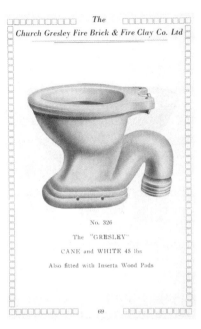

Church Gresley Firebrick and Fireclay Co. Ltd. around 1930

Benjamin Robinson and Eli Massey began the manufacture at Church Gresley of sanitary earthenware (W.C.s, traps and connected products) importing, mainly from Cornwall, much of the white clay they needed. In pottery, T.G. Green bought from Henry Wileman the pottery which had originally been founded by Leedham. Also, near the railway line at Woodville was Bretby Art Pottery (Henry Tooth, 1883).

Because of the weight and volume of sanitary pipes, access to good transport was essential for their marketing. The construction of the Swadlincote-Woodville-Moira railway loop, passing through clay-mining districts with pottery kilns using local fuel, encouraged makers of pipes such as Wragg to commence and expand production. The railway ran past a succession of clay product entrepreneurs: Robinsons, Ensors, Albion (founded in 1872 by Henry Knowles and Hosea Tugby) and Wragg.

A number of ancillary industries gained from the success of pottery production. There was an intimate connection between crate shops and output from the kilns. Hazel from Herefordshire and osiers from the Middle Trent flood-plain were used to make the rectangular wicker-type crates, packed with straw, that would safeguard either water-closets or delicate china in transit over rough ground. Most cratemakers were on or near to the road from Swadlincote to Woodville.[27] There were also rope makers in the area to serve the pottery trade. In the early part of the 19th century, horse-drawn carts had taken ware by road to Horninglow, where the crates would be transferred to the Trent-Mersey Canal, often for eventual export via Liverpool.

SOUTH DERBYSHIRE CLAYS

Terminology of early local clay industry
a) Yellow clay for brick-making ('tough Tom')
b) 'Pot clay' (with sufficient iron content could make Rockingham ware)

c) Fireclay for firebricks and refractories

d) 'Blue billy' from Dorset and Devon for blue bricks. The glaze for the bricks came by barrel from a mill near Bretby Iron nodules from open clay holes would be picked out by hand

Holmes classification (1959)[28]

1. Fireclays with high alumina and minimum iron content; went into kiln bottoms
2. Seatearths with a high silica content used for making pipes that were salt-glazed
3. Fusible clays from Keuper Marl and Coal Measure clays (for bricks and terra-cotta)
4. Imported clays
   (a) cane firing, clays from other coal and ironstone areas
   (b) white burning clay [Cornwall supplied ball clay and kaolin, to which flint was added]

The distribution of clay workings in the South Derbyshire coalfield is delimited almost exactly by the Boothorpe Fault on the east and on the west side less exactly by the Dicky Gobbler outcrop.[29] A geological study has offered to delineate by map references the irregularly-shaped area containing active and recently worked pottery clay pits: 1. Church Gresley (SK 2918), 2. Swadlincote (SK 3019), 3. Blackfordby (SK 3318), 4. Moira (SK 3216), 5. Overseal (SK 2915).[30]

SOUTH DERBYSHIRE CLAY INDUSTRY

Share of employment by product[31]

%

53 Pipes and refractories
24 Pottery
14 Bricks and terra-cotta
9 Sanitary ware

Donington Sanitary Pipe and Firebrick Co. Ltd.
Firebrick works at Church Gresley 1918

Donington Clay Pit No. 1 with brickworks in the distance 1918

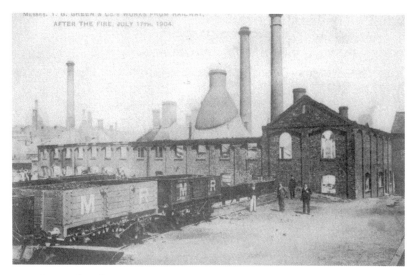

T.G. Green Church Gresley Pottery Works after a major fire on 17th July, 1904.

© Courtesy of Magic Attic Archives

Some of the firms engaged in more than one category; eg. a pipe manufacturer may also have produced a substantial quantity of bricks

POTTERY MASTERS

The pottery entrepreneurs included some interesting characters who though not local to the area became very much part of Church Gresley society.

One of the early potters to adopt the area as his home was Moses Jones, born in 1769. A native of Mold in Flintshire, Jones came to Church Gresley in 1793 with an interest in religion and, by using local minerals, manufactured articles for which there was a market. A brief partnership with his brother was dissolved and Moses went on to found a pancheon works on the north of the Common, with clay from beneath it and fuel available from the several local pits or from peat found in the spinney at Spinney Corner (Woodhouse Junction). Moses himself made the bricks with which to build his potworks.

The family was large and one of its descendants was Walter Jones of Swadlincote, founder of a flourishing music business. Moses was influential in establishing the Wesleyan Methodist meeting house at the Top of the Hill, where the first services were held in a cottage near to his home.

Of a later generation was T.G. Green (1826-1902)[32] founder of a famous and long lived company. Like Jones, he was not a local man.

Thomas Goodwin Green, born in Boston, Lincolnshire, emigrated to Australia. On his return he bought the 'Flint Mill' from Grey (Gray) – an agent for John Mammatt of Ashby, who held a lease on the clays under Gresley Common from the Lord of the Manor and who already worked clay pits there. In 1864, Green took over from Henry Wileman the old Church Gresley Pottery that had been in existence since 1790, later known as Green's Top Works. Green, having started with yellow ware, moved to white earthenware, sinking a shaft to get his own coal supply for a new Lower (or Bottom) works. This was built on two large fields belonging to the first intake abstracted from Common land. Clay, besides what was dug from the Common that lay outside the works gate, was now brought in from Hartshorne, Ticknall and Boothorpe. Wages were not high but in the mid 1880s, for making daisy plates, it was possible to earn 14s in a good week. 'T.G.' died in 1902, a long time before the famous Cornish ware pattern of the 1930s was introduced.

WORKING IN THE POTTERY INDUSTRY

Although less painful than the struggles of the miners, the pottery industry saw its share of owner/union negotiations. Representatives of eight sanitary ware firms met to negotiate prices with the Potters Union in January 1905, the resulting agreement being written by the Sharpe Bros' secretary, and distributed to those attending: 1- Morrison Ingram, 2- Nadin

At the potter's wheel. Richard E. Hull, (the author's father) sanitary presser
at the works of Benjamin Robinson Ltd., 1939

© K.A. Hull

Parker, 3- B. Robinson, 4- C.W.Outram, 5- Goodman and
Adams, 6- Mansfield Bros., 7- Sharpe Bros., 8- Cutforth. But
this, the second attempt to agree prices, collapsed – as the
first such move had done – as soon as one firm attempted to
seize more trade by undercutting the agreed prices.

For the ordinary worker, the wages and working
conditions left much to be desired. Richard Edwin Hull, like
his father in law Joseph Payne, (see Chapter 14) worked in a
clay-based industry. The clay dust involved in sweeping up a
potter's shop was a known industrial hazard to employees,
Richard's own father died young from 'potter's rot'. A
journeyman-potter in 1910, Richard worked as a sanitary
presser for the small family firm of Benjamin Robinson and
was paid on piece-rates with average weekly earnings in 1910
of only 13s 6d per week. Things improved with the graduation
to making full W.C. ware and by 1924 take-home pay for a $5^1/2$
day week had risen to an average of £3 11s per week, but short-
time work during the depression that followed reduced

189

earnings to a weekly average of £2 10s 9d in 1933.

Employees like Richard, who lived near enough, could walk home for their dinner hour. For others with more distant homes it was necessary for one of the family's children-during school break-to carry dinner to their father. This was by means of a 'snap-basket' a wicker basket usually containing a meal in a basin wrapped around with a cloth or large male handkerchief.

Clay based industry

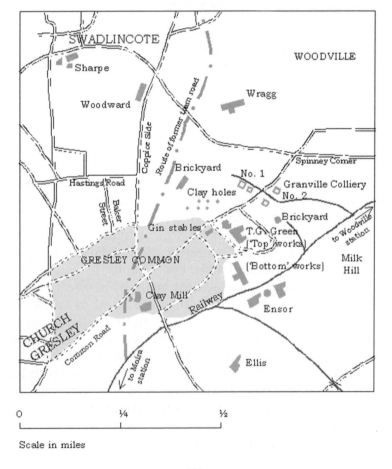

1   VCH Derbys. Vol II.
2   Parliamentary Papers, Agriculture Vol. 7, p. 552.
3   Recorded at the Corn Exchange, Derby, for the Market Herald.
4   Parliamentary Papers. Preamble to the Report of the Select Committee on Agriculture, Irish University Press, p. xii.
5   Ibid.
6   Ibid.
7   Pigot's Derbyshire Directory 1821-22: Transcript of Sections relating to Repton & Gresley Hundred, South Derbyshire Genealogical Resources, 2000; Glover, op. cit., vol II, p. 162.
8   Holmes, W.D., The Leicestershire and South Derbyshire Coalfield: The Coal Mining Industry, East Midland Geographer Vol. 10, December 1958, p. 19.
9   Phillipps Charters, op. cit. no. 302.
10 Phillipps Charters no. 328.
11 PRO E/178/618.
12 Phillipps Charters no. 329.
13 Ibid.
14 VCH Leics. Vol. III, p. 33.
15 Gresley Papers, Box 4, item no. 31.
16 Beaumont, P., History of the Moira Collieries, Bemrose & Sons: Derby & London, 1919, p. 1.
17 Farey, op. cit. Vol. I.
18 National Coal Board, E. Midl. Division, courtesy Maurice Hall, 1961.
19 Griffin, A.R., The British Coalmining Industry: Retrospect and Prospect, Moorland Publishing Co: Buxton, 1977, p. 76.
20 Green, H., Child Labour in the Coal Mines of Nottinghamshire and Derbyshire in the 19th century: Extracts from the Reports of Commissioners, 1842, Derbyshire Archaeological Society, 1936, p. 10.
21 M. Hall, archive material.
22 Beaumont, op. cit.., p. 8.
23 Chandler, T.J., Communications and a Coalfield: a study in the Leicestershire and South Derbyshire Coalfield Transactions, Institute of British Geographers, 1957, p. 168.
24 Eckersley, G., local historian – archive material.
25 Pilkington, James, A view of the present state of Derbyshire, 2 vols., William Marriott: Derby, 1803.
26 Holmes, W.D., The Leicestershire and South Derbyshire Coalfield: The Clay Industry, East Midland Geographer Vol. 12, December 1959, p. 10.
27 White, P.M. & Storer, J.W., Around the Wooden Box, 1984, History of Woodville industries.
28 Holmes, op. cit. The Clay Industry; M. Hull.
29 Holmes, ibid., pp. 9, 12.
30 Sylvester-Bradley, P.C. & Ford, T.D. (eds.), The Geology of the East Midlands, Leicester University Press: Leicester, 1968.
31 Holmes, op. cit., p. 12.
32 White and Storer; op. cit.; M. Hull.

CHAPTER 13

THE TRANSPORT REVOLUTION

CANALS

The solid fuels and ores directly relevant to the Industrial Revolution were just the sort of cargo suited to shipment by water. There were many physical obstacles facing the canal builder in the Midlands that would necessitate the use of locks, so increasing the cost of construction, but developments in materials analysis and engineering science produced rapid advances in linking producer and consumer.

Britain was fortunate in having a wealth of natural resources, but they required bulk carriage. Where coal was needed at a distant destination, there was going to be a huge gain from delivering it by barge instead of by road. Whereas it had needed eight horses hitched to a heavy road wagon to pull a load of six tons, one beast was able to haul a 25-ton barge by canal, or canalised river.[1] The East Midlands region was blessed with many rivers that had once been invasion routes, but were now to help in carrying important minerals. The significance of improvements to rivers has been shown in a study by W.L. Jones. He calculated that, of all the miles of waterways navigable nationwide in 1800, one third had been canalised between 1600 and 1760.[2]

In the area of the Middle Trent in the northern section of South Derbyshire, there was ample room for the river, downstream from its confluence with the Dove, first to have meandered over a flood plain and then to have been brought up to the standard of a considerable carrier. Above Wilden Ferry, the Trent had been made navigable, under an Act of 1699, to Fleetstones Bridge, near Burton. The main promoter then was Lord William Paget, a local coal owner who, with the promise of ample traffic, raised sufficient capital to build locks on the river at King's Mills and Burton Mills, with the cuts and basin necessary to handle commercial traffic coming from both Derbyshire and Staffordshire. In 1762 control of traffic on the river was leased to the Burton Canal Company but in 1766 there were complaints from the Staffordshire merchants using the river of 'Monopoly in the Hands of a few Persons' affecting traffic between Burton and Wilden Ferry. Added to the natural hazards of 'Floods in Winter and ... Shallows in Summer,'[3] there had been under-investment by the operators.

BEFORE THE RAILWAY AGE

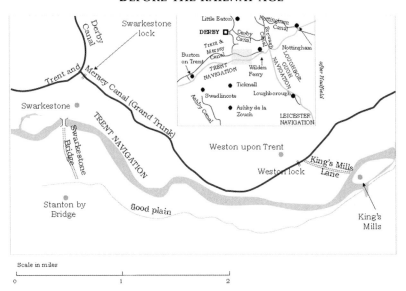

Tramroads and canals had a special relationship; the tram-road's habitual role being to carry, from its quay or wharf, bulk minerals derived from mine, quarry or separation plant. In view of the tonnage involved and the weight of horse-drawn wagons designed each to carry two tons or more, it was necessary to have a properly surveyed, engineered and constructed rail-bed. James Brindley, canal

Tramways of the Canal Era[4]

Date of tramway opening	Canal	Junction point of canal and tramway	Feeder terminals	Principal cargo	Tramway length in miles
1799-1802	Ashby	Willesley Basin	Ticknall (legs): Staunton Harold / Cloud Hill / Lount	Lime / ditto / ditto / ditto	8·5 / 3·75 (Cloud branch)
d1827		'Cut End' (west of Spring Cottage)	Church Gresley / Swadlincote	Coal / ditto	3 (total mileage, Swadlincote to Cut End)
1795-1804	Derby	Little Eaton	Smith Houses (continuation by private lines): Denby / Kilburn / Salterwood Coal	Coal	4 / 2

The narrow boat 'Apple' on the Trent and Mersey Canal at Barrow-on-Trent
© Courtesy of Derby Museums and Art Gallery

The Trent at Kings Mills looking towards Weston-on-Trent
from an 18th century engraving

The Trent and Mersey Canal at Weston-on-Trent around 1905

Remains of the Harpur-Crewe limeyard, Ticknall

© 1989 David Birt

designer for the Potteries, who died in 1772, had given advice on a route to be taken north-westwards through Derbyshire from the Trent-Mersey canal bypassing Derby itself. The Derby Canal and associated tramroad to Denby that followed were the joint work of Benjamin Outram, surveyor and engineer and William Jessop, who had been a consultant engineer for Trent Navigation, with a remit to improve the river below Wilden Ferry.[5] The Little Eaton line (called locally 'the gangway') continued to be improved along its single track, with more and more passing points added, until in 1825 there were nine of them on the way to Denby and the other collieries. As each box of coal carried on its wagon reached Little Eaton, it would be lifted by crane onto a barge.[6]

Coals from Derbyshire were the basis for fiercely competitive canal-building southwards from the many collieries north-east of Derby. Coal was required for new or converted mills or for office and domestic heating in Midland cities and the South of England. There was one natural artery of trade, the Trent, that was improved below Wilden Ferry after 1783, when the Trent Navigation Company first met. Important traffic links that followed valleys tributary to the main river had earlier been opened: the Soar Navigation, (August 1778) and the Erewash Canal (December 1779).[7] By 1785, Derbyshire mines, using mainly the Erewash-Soar route, were supplying about half of the coal used in Leicestershire, Rutland and Northamptonshire.[8] Developments in the main Derbyshire field were of great interest to land and coal owners and investors in the south of the county. Link canals, often fed by tramways, were planned to run from north-east of Derby to the Trent. An Act to create a Derby Canal was passed on 7 May 1793, dividends being fixed at eight per cent.[9]

Coal, though providing much of the early canal tonnage, was not the only bulk cargo. Hadfield lists the freight carried by the Derby Canal, in 1839, in order of tonnage: 'coal, stone,

Twyford Ferry remained in use until 1963

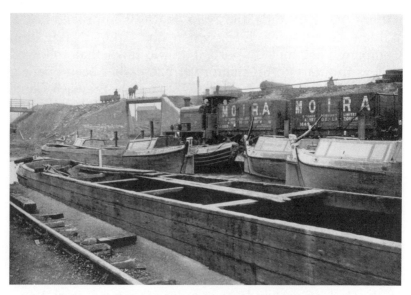

Reservoir Colliery canal boats 1918

corn and cement.' There were extraordinarily quick profits to be made by shareholders of the specialist companies, the most spectacular being the Erewash. From $2^1/2$ per cent in 1783, its dividend spurted to 20 per cent in 1787, 30 per cent in 1794 and 42 per cent in 1824. Company earnings were derived from tolls levied per ton of freight: from the flat rate of 6d per ton (the Erewash toll) the company could afford to pay a fee to the operator taking the freight forward on the next stage to its final destination.

Canals had become an important part of the business scene and of popular culture. Any new project attracted interest from a wide geographical area. In the earliest days of the Derby Canal people from Northampton, Harborough and various parts of Leicestershire who had arrived in Derby on 9 August 1792 'with the supposed intention' of buying shares in the Derby Canal were turned away, so it was said 'with chagrin and disappointment' from a private committee meeting. At this time a respected engineer, Outram, was surveying a project (not taken up) for an extension of the canal southwards to Newhall and Swadlincote.[x]

THE ASHBY CANAL

The men who met at Ashby-de-la-Zouch on 30 August 1792 knew that canals already built had been highly profitable, with Coventry Canal shares, for instance, earning eight per cent and improving. Within a decade they had trebled in value. The proposal before the Ashby meeting was to connect the limeworks at Ticknall to Ashby Woulds and 'from there to unite with the Coventry Canal at or near Griff'. Among the canal's supporters were gentlemen and aristocrats from both Derbyshire and Leicestershire: the Earl of Stamford (owner of the limeworks at Cloud Hill and Breedon) the Earl Ferrers and Mr. Francis Burdett of Foremark. Two titled sympathisers were to give important help: Lord Rawdon of Donnington Park (after whom a local colliery was to be named) and the Hon. Penn Assheton Curzon of Gopsall, a Leicester M.P. These were people regionally significant as landowners and industrialists, who felt they could not afford to miss participation in a promising enterprise.

Success depended on the logistics of plans to link this relatively small operation with larger concerns already carrying loads to destinations as far as London. One tactic designed to tie coal producers to this route was a low introductory toll of only 1d a ton per mile for coal ($^1/_2$d for limestone).[9]

The securing of freight and markets was the essence of canal, as of any transport, business. There needed to be constant checks on the availability of money to go ahead with expensive projects. Highly competent engineers had long since shown canals to be technically feasible, only for money supply to become difficult during the wars with the French. There had been protests in Parliament in 1781 when the Government had raised loans at $5^1/_2$ per cent interest.[12] The rate continued to rise and more than doubled by the turn of the century. There was pressure from coal owners to agree the projected canal's route, length and dimensions and despite the costs of construction having escalated, the enterprise was agreed at last, and opened on 19 April 1804. It was decided not to have a canal extension to the limeworkings on Derbyshire border: their output was to be shifted by tramroad. The total cost (of £166,322) for the combined canal and tramroads was over six times the original estimate of £27,317[13] for a canal from Ashby to a junction at Griff with the Coventry system.

The coal trade was the making of the canal and the creation, or enlargement, of considerable fortunes. The Rawdon pit was opened within a short distance of the canal in 1821 and the Church Gresley Colliery's first shaft sunk in 1829. Between these dates a tramway had been built across the intervening ground, including Gresley Common,

The "Clock Warehouse" Shardlow on the Trent and Mersey Canal

reaching Swadlincote by 1827.[14]

More toll revenue was now being taken by the canal company and an increase in traffic paying toll, but John Wilkes of Measham, a coal owner and major shareholder in the canals, advised that it was necessary to import coal freight from Warwick and Staffordshire in exchange for lime contributed by the tramways and then carried to Birmingham on neighbouring canals.

In an interesting attempt to widen their market, the company agreed in 1816 to a private group's proposal to put a passenger-carrying boat on the canal. The group had to pay 3d a mile toll; the horses were not to go faster than a walking pace and 'merchandise' carried by the passenger boats was not to exceed 50 hundredweight.[15]

The company paid its first dividend in 1828 (in respect of 1827), which was a major relief to investors, given that the share issue price of £113 had at one time fallen to £10. Investment in such relatively small companies was not a matter for the faint-hearted; but payment of a first dividend

Date from which toll operated	Canal/river	Cargo	Toll per ton	
1794	Ashby Canal	Coal, lime slate	$1\frac{1}{4}^{d}$	
		Most other traffic	2^{d}	
1797	Leicester Navigation	Coal	$1^{s}8^{d}$	
1778	Loughboro Navigation	Coal	1/-	Important outlets southwards from Derbyshire
1792		All cargo	$1^{s}6^{d}$	
1792	Nottingham Canal		$4\frac{1}{2}^{d}$ and $\frac{1}{2}^{d}$ per ton-mile (1/- maximum)	

Reduction in tolls.
Coal from south Derbyshire or the Derby-Notts Coalfield for the London market had to use several elements of canal network. Tolls on the Oxford Canal were reduced in 1829 from 2ˢ9ᵈ to 1ˢ6ᵈ

pulled in 1828 was £2 per £113 share, and this was doubled the next year.[16]

Further north, there was a business-cum-leisure venture larger than the Ashby canal's. From Swarkestone, at its junction with the Trent, on the Derby Canal was a 'Market boat, decked over, with seats, and a fireplace, for the accommodation of passengers.' The boat left Swarkestone every Friday morning to carry market people to Derby, at 6d each, leaving Derby again at 4 o'clock for Swarkestone.[17]

Traffic, faster than on the conventional barge, passed westwards into Staffordshire from Shardlow along the Trent and Mersey, using flyboats. On the other hand, the Trent itself was worked at low speeds by the Burton Boat Company's nineteen barges. There were times in drier seasons when cargo had to be almost halved to cope with the shallows.[18] Things were different downstream from the Cavendish Bridge, though one had to find transport to Nottingham to catch the steam packet service starting from there for Gainsborough; Fares, with refreshments, were 5s and 8s 6d. All this was to change with the appearance, long-threatened, of a working competitor – the Midland Counties Railway between Nottingham and Derby that opened on 4 June 1839, seven years after the benchmark opening of the Leicester-Swannington line.

As an example of the handling of great profit in the canal business, Trent and Mersey Canal Company £200 shares were, by an Act of Parliament, split into units of £100, each of which four years later stood at £840. In that year, 1806, the dividend was 40 per cent, rising to 45 per cent in 1811 and 75 per cent in 1822. The company was a power in the land and it was to them that the Shardlow Parish Council turned for help towards the relief of its parish poor. Shardlow, an important trans-shipment point on the canal, saw its population rise from 580 in 1802 to 1301 in 1841, falling back to 842 in 1891.[19]

ROADS

The early medieval roads still reflected the Roman road pattern. In South Derbyshire the Roman Ryknield Street followed the left bank of the Trent in the direction of the Roman Deventium (known later by its British name of Little Chester, one mile north of the centre of modern Derby).

There were important cross-country connections belonging to religious houses – notably the one joining Burton Abbey and Gresley Priory with Merevale Abbey in Warwickshire. The route south eastwards from Stapenhill through Castle Gresley and Overseal involved crossing Seal Brook at Acresford and likewise the Mease at a point liable to flooding.

Most of the early 'roads' were tracks cleared through woods, thickets and shrubland, but they were nevertheless crucial for grain and timber deliveries. Some important movements involved delivery of produce offered as payment for tithes. In the southern and northernmost parts

The Toll Gate at Woodville around 1906

Church Gresley Firebrick and Fire Clay Co. Ltd. The Fleet, around 1930

of this region, the most valuable material handled in the Newhall-Swadlincote-Woodville area was coal.

T.J. Chandler[20] describes how coal was carried from the South Derbyshire-Leicester-shire coalfield in panniers slung across the backs of horses and mules that had been loaned from local farmers for work during the winter months.

This traffic was busiest on the Ashby turnpike to Leicester. The corresponding turnpike from Ashby to Burton opened in 1753, connecting with Horninglow in Staffordshire where there were wharves on the Trent and Mersey (afterwards the Grand Union Canal). The Grand Union (completed in 1777) was opened to freight that reached the canal via the Burton-Ashby turnpike and then the Newton-Repton road, raised above flood level, that led to the Willington ferry. With the rapid growth of pottery output in the Swadlincote area, there was an increased traffic of horse-drawn crated ware to the Grand Union Canal wharves at Horninglow.

The next bridge over the Trent below Burton was at Swarkestone, dating from the 14th century and accessible from the Ticknall, Stanton, and Melbourne road.

Bridges were all-important in attracting traffic: The Cavendish Bridge, built in 1760 half a mile south east of Shardlow, was used by the post road from Manchester to London (later the A6) to cross the Trent. It could happen that between turnpikes, there were large areas of difficult country with poor communications. But given the impetus of a new addition to production and trade, it became worthwhile to consider cross links such as the route to run across Gresley Common to Castle Gresley from the Burton-Ashby to the Burton-Atherstone turnpike. The proposal to build the link had been put forward in 1833 and agreed by the Lord of the Manor, Sir Roger Gresley.

There was a direct connection between road improvement and the growth of local industry (both

Swadlincote Bus Station 1945

Remains of Cavendish Bridge, washed away in the great flood, 1947

Willington Bridge, toll bridge
constructed in 1839

DCHQ

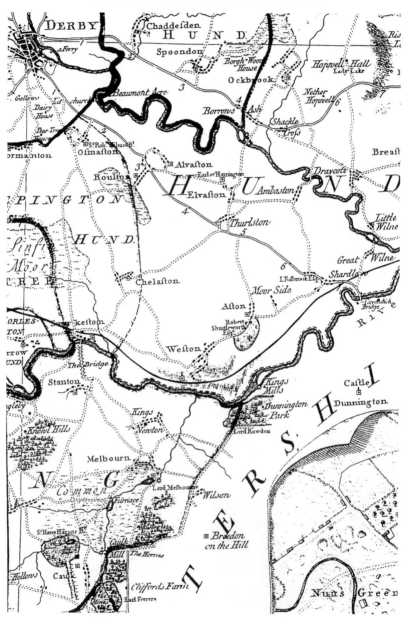

BURDETT MAP OF DERBYSHIRE 1791

extractive and manufacturing), and it was also found that better roads had promoted trade. There were critics – notably the traveller and observer Arthur Young, who had written in 1769: 'All the sensible people had attributed the dearness of their country to the turnpike roads, and reason speaks the truth of their opinion...make but a turnpike road through their country and all the cheapness vanishes at once'.[21]

RAILWAYS

Whilst an important element of the industrial revolution, the canal system that had performed so mightily was superseded in much of Britain, and in most of its functions, by a new method of transport. The railway grew out of the adaptation to rail of Trevithick's road vehicle, driven by steam which first ran on Cornish roads in 1801. Railway engines, when developed and refined by the Stephensons, produced vehicles that could haul loads much greater than the biggest barge had been able to manage.

The local men of property who had financed the Midland canals had now to take account of the railway's potential to bring them profit. Wherever a canal could go between Trent, Soar and Mease, a railway could surely be driven, and possibly with far fewer physical complications. The Leicester-Swannington line, surveyed by George Stephenson and constructed by his son Robert, was opened in 1832 to serve the Leicestershire coalfield. Its extension to Burton via Ashby, Moira and Gresley opened on the first day of March 1849.

There was popular excitement at what was correctly identified as a crucially important social development, the organisation of which had entailed the assemblage of a massive array of machinery, materials and men. Many of the navvies (originally 'navigators') had worked on canals. A good number of them came from Ireland, but many in the Middle Trent region were originally farm labourers,

Church Gresley (built 1899)

New Church Gresley (built 1900). These locomotives were owned and
worked by the Moira Colliery Co. that operated Church Gresley Colliery

combining harvesting with navvying. Some found it possible eventually to work full-time on the burgeoning new network, earning from 15s to 16s 6d even in a bad year, such as 1843, and 22s 6d to 24s in the good year of 1846.[22] The most graphic account of the physical impact of the coming of a railway is in Dickens' "Dombey and Son". It is based on that author's observation when, as a resident at the southern end of the main line that led from Birmingham to London's Euston Station, he saw the new railway devouring the playground where he had gone to school. In South Derbyshire, the railroad required the recruitment of large numbers of staff to service passenger movements and, more importantly, the carriage of freight. The chief local resources relevant to the role of the railway as carrier were coal and other minerals. In the local manufactured goods sector of railway business William Bass's brewery had been in operation at Burton since 1777. The Gresley line, an extension to the Leicester-Swannington base, was built when the economy was emerging from a depression that had lasted from 1837 to 1842,[23] during which there had been a record level of business failures and unemployment.

Coal, for more than a generation, had been carried through Derbyshire by the canals and canalised rivers that were now functional competitors with the railway. Landowners, coalowners and country gentlemen had together promoted and financed the canals with themselves or their nominees in place on the canal boards. When, in March 1830 the Ashby Canal Company received in committee its 'first word about railways'[24] it did not take long to appreciate the commercial significance of the new transport form. Railways contained within them the magical element of Progress. This was a second (communications-based) phase of the industrial revolution. To survive, canals lowered their tolls and the Ashby Canal Company obtained agreement with Grand Union to reduce fees payable for shipping coal forward to the London market; and still the railways pushed ahead.

It was inevitable that the men of property, given a choice of investments, would place new – and probably borrowed – capital into railway enterprises. There was nothing to prevent canal companies, their coffers full of past profits, from investing in the transport form of the future. In 1830 a forward-looking Derby Canal Company had commissioned plans of their own for railway building.

A prime mover in the market was George Hudson, the 'Railway King,' who, after starting as a linen draper in York, collected directorships of several companies. Hudson, a player in and manipulator of the market, became Chairman of the Midland Railway, but was eventually ruined after being exposed for financial malpractice. Whilst still in his post in the mid-1840s he worked to safeguard the Company's future against any possible competitor. The Ashby Canal was purchased in 1845 for £110,000. With both railway and canal in their possession the Midland had moved against prospective competitor rail lines to Bedford; and a link from Atherstone and Ashby-de-la-Zouch to Burton.[25] What was at stake was the coal trade from South Derbyshire and Leicestershire.

At the northern end of South Derbyshire, engineering and business activity rapidly gathered pace with the opening in 1840 by the Midland Railway of a strategic route for the delivery of coal to the London basin. It led from Derby to Rugby by way of Trent Station, Loughborough and Leicester. There followed the opening in 1847 of the Erewash Valley Railway between Codnor Park and Trent Station.[26] The opening of the railway line to Leicester drastically reduced business in carrying Derbyshire coal on the parallel canal route that followed the Soar Valley. 'Canal mania' had brought an increase in the price of Soar and Leicester Navigation shares from an initial £1421 8s to £4950 in 1824. There followed a steady decline to £3000 in 1830 and a much sharper fall to £530 in 1850. The speculator's skill had lain in knowing when to sell, when to buy and into which stock.[27i]

From Derby, three trunk lines diverged. From Trent Junction, there were four: to Derby, Sheffield, Nottingham and Leicester. Competitors would strive either to forestall or react to an initiative. Every modification of route required an Act of Parliament – one reason why a Midland line to St. Pancras took until 1868 to open. The marvellous cast-iron roof to the terminal station was built with Derbyshire material by the Butterley Company and survives today as a masterpiece of Victorian engineering. Another local iron-works that prospered with the railway boom was Andrew Handyside, manufacturer of a similar roof for the Midland's Glasgow Station. He had had an iron works in Derby since 1818 and the railway greatly helped his business to grow. In the second half of the century, his Britannia Iron Works was supplying high-grade castings to the Midland's Derby works. Bemrose, a local stationer, won a contract to supply

Level crossing and signal box by the side of Swadlincote East station on the Woodville loop. c.1905. Chimneys of Ault's Pottery on the left of the picture and of Cartwright Colliery (Shoddy Pit) on the right

© Courtesy of Magic Attic Archives

the Midland with stationery and print its timetables.[28]

RAIL AND COLLIERY CONNECTIONS

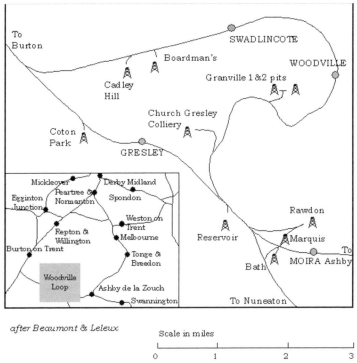

after Beaumont & Leleux

Scale in miles

An important addition to the railway on the South Derbyshire coalfield was the loop to the Burton Ashby line that opened as far as Swadlincote on 1 June 1864. This was extended to Woodville on 1 May 1883 and continued back to the Burton-Ashby line, joining it between Swiss Cottage and Swains Park. The loop finally lost its passenger services on 6 October 1947,[29] but during its life had played an essential part in the operation of the local coal and pottery industries. As well as regular services, the line had passenger excursion trains, that could be joined at Woodville or Swadlincote and regular football 'specials' for Peartree, the station for Derby County's Baseball Ground.

215

The steam railway's arrival had been a major social event, with wide cultural implications. Thomas Cook, born in Melbourne in 1808, who became a Baptist missionary, applied to the Midland Railway Company to run an excursion on 5 July 1841 to a temperance meeting in Lough-borough: it was Britain's first special outing by rail. There followed further excursions, depending on a promoter being able to fill the train, and in 1856 Thomas Cook ran his first Grand Tour of Europe.

On a more mundane level, natives of Melbourne and Swadlincote, instead of walking to an annual fair – or as well as doing so – could soon take day or half-day excursions to shop in Derby. The rising population of the industrial south of the region was, in a 'good' year, able to venture further afield. Before the First World War, the radius of family travel had reached the coast and the children of a generation once tied to its place of birth discovered the sea at Blackpool and Llandudno. East Midland accents were more and more heard on the sands as the Lincolnshire coast became available to holidaymakers from South Derbyshire. From Burton they needed to change trains at Derby and stations at Lincoln – a consequence of the competitive, multiple-owner development of the railway system.

Summer was a busy time for excursion trains on the Woodville Loop. The Burton Mail in August 1898, reported the departure to Liverpool by special train of the staff of Woodward & Co (Swadlincote), followed the next day, by an even more impressive enterprise:

Three trains were necessary to convey the heads of departments, office staff, and artisans connected with the firms of Messrs. Green and Co. (Church Gresley), John Knowles and Co. (Woodville) and Messrs. The Woodville Sanitary Pipe Co. Quite seventeen hundred proceeded to Blackpool, and a fair proportion went on to the Isle of Man.

THE BURTON AND ASHBY LIGHT RAILWAY

Running between Burton and Ashby, owned by the Midland Railway and using cars decorated on their side panels with the Company's coat-of-arms, the Light Railway was opened between Burton and Swadlincote on 13 June 1906. Service to Ashby started on 2 July of the same year. The great degree of local interest and involvement shown by the total of 45,000 passengers using the railway in its first week suggested a major change in travel patterns, but this situation was, to the disappointment of many, relatively short-lived, and by 1918 the service was running at a loss.[30] Motive power for the line was distributed from a power station using diesel driven generators located near to Swadlincote railway station. On a fine day, a ride on the top deck of the open cars, for instance between Newhall and the Burton road, could be a most pleasant experience. The gauge of the lines was 3ft 6ins and driving controls at both ends of a car were necessary on the single track. A conductor worked the reversible arm at a terminus to pick up current from the overhead cable.

It did not prove possible to live with the competition from a powerful new rival in the shape of regional buses: principally those of the Birmingham Red Motor Bus Company.

Burton-Ashby Light Railway. Tramcar in open country 1909.
The service closed in 1927

© L. Payne

A Burton-bound tram outside the Postman's house in Newhall

A view in Ashby Road, Woodville around 1907

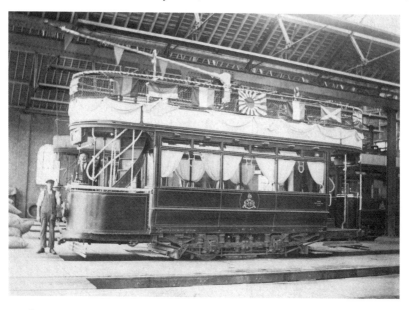

The Burton and Ashby Light Railway Wedding Car in the Tram Depot
around 1923

The Swadlincote United Methodist Free Church Treat goes by tram in 1908

The last service of the Light Railway ran on 19 February 1927. It had been quite a short life. After the closure the "Midland Red" bus company took over and greatly extended the old tramway routes. Motor transport had developed fast since the invention, in 1885, by the Germans, Daimler and Benz, of a petrol driven car. It rapidly affected movement patterns so

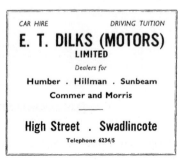

that colliers who had once tramped to Rawdon and Marquis pits were being conveyed there by hired bus before 1939. Not long after the end of the war they began to use their own cars or shared transport. Meanwhile local councils fretted over the contributions they were going to have to make towards road building and maintenance.

1 Roy Porter, op. cit., p. 208.
2 Floud & Closkey, op. cit. Vol. I, p. 66.
3 Hadfield, Charles, Canals of the West Midlands, David & Charles: Newton Abbott, 1985. p. 17.
4 Hadfield, op. cit. East Midlands, p. 66 & p. 77.
5 Hadfield, op. cit. East Midlands, p. 45.
6 Ibid, p. 69.
7 Chandler, op. cit., p. 165.
8 Ibid.
9 Hadfield, op. cit. East Midlands, p. 68.
10 Ibid., p. 67.
11 Ibid, p. 148.
12 Ashton, T.S., The Industrial Revolution 1760-1830, Oxford University Press: London, 1948., p. 100.
13 Hadfield, op. cit. East Midlands, p. 150.
14 Ibid, p. 155.
15 Ibid.
16 Ibid, p. 153.
17 Ibid, p. 69, quoting Farey.
18 Hadfield, op. cit. East Midlands, p. 77.
19 Ibid, p. 76.
20 Chandler, T.J., Communications and a Coalfield: a study in the Leicestershire and South Derbyshire Coalfield. Transactions, Institute of British Geographers, 1957, pp. 163-172, p. 165.
21 Quoted by Hayek, F.A. (ed.), Capitalism and the Historians, Routledge & Kegan Paul: London, 1954, p. 147.
22 Harrison, J.F.C., Early Victorian Britain, 1832-51, Fontana: London, 1979, pp. 49-50.
23 Ibid., pp. 24-5.
23 Hadfield, op. cit. East Midlands, p. 156.
25 Ibid., p. 211.
26 Chandler, op. cit., p. 170.
27 Ibid.
28 Leleux, Robin, A Regional History of the Railways of Great Britain, Vol. 9: The East Midlands, David St. John Thomas: Newton Abbot, 1984, p. 166.
29 Harrison, op.cit.,, p. 103.
30 Hillier, op. cit., p. 83.

CHAPTER 14

JOSEPH PAYNE:

A CLAY WORKER'S PROGRESS

The pace of change in South Derbyshire through the 19th and early 20th centuries was unrelenting. To put into context the environmental and social changes that took place it is useful to look at the life experiences of individuals who lived through these times.

Joseph Payne, was born in 1853 on Commonside, Church Gresley, where his father William kept a beer shop, the Robin Hood. A bright boy, Joseph was sent by his parents to the National School that was financed substantially by the

Joseph Payne, left of picture, taken in Manchester, where he was married in 1875 to Ann Waring
© J. Payne

Lily Payne in 1908, aged 25. She had travelled with her father to the Isle of Man in 1894
© J. Payne

National (Church of England) Society. He had to leave before the age of 10 to help with his father's business based on the public house, the Potters Arms, along with which went two fields behind the works of T.G. Green, the pottery manufacturer. As it appeared to everyone, after Joseph left school, that he deserved some more educational help, William took advantage of a partial solution, whereby one of his customers would work off a drinking debt to give his son some basic private tuition.

In the Payne family, there was a well-established fruit and vegetable round, using produce from the smallholding as well as what was bought in from markets as far away as Derby and Uttoxeter. Animals could be turned onto the Common to graze and there was hay to be mown from the two fields. In 1875 Joseph married the orphaned Ann Waring after they had exchanged letters whilst she was working in Lancashire.

ANN WARING TO JOSEPH PAYNE

Ann writes from Lancashire to Joseph in Church Gresley.

Chilwell Manor
August 15, 1874

Ann writes:

I was sorry you were disopointed in not coming to see me on your wakes but I hope you enjoyed your self without me. I suppose it has been a grand fete this year but it was very bad wether for you all. I thougt of you and wished I had been ther. I shall come over in October without I come at Christmas. I have sent you this portrait as you hoped I should send you one so you will have some thing for to think of me now but I don't think that they much like me. I should very much like to have yours but praps it is to much truble for you to have them taken, but I shall make you happit when I come. I don't know if I am going to leave Manchester and live at home but I think I should rather stay where I was. I

think you will be tired in reading this letter. I must now conclude with the fondest love and remain your true lover.
A. Waring

('wakes': a family holiday period)

Ann, whose parents had both died young, married Joseph in Manchester Cathedral on 9 March 1875. 'Home' which she mentions in her letter was in Leicestershire, where her mother, born in Packington, had returned to remarry. She had died giving birth, to stillborn twin girls.

Joseph, uneasy over his association with the liquor trade, sold the Potters Arms, and became a collier at the nearby Granville pit, where he joined the union and supported its demand for a fairer deal for the men.

In 1892-3 there was a protracted strike leading to police being billeted for the duration in the colliery office. Ann Payne, along with wives of other striking miners, was arrested and charged with trespass and stealing company property – a legal definition for the pieces of coal that had been discarded along with ashes and other waste and tipped onto the colliery bank. The result of their appearance in court is not known, but a letter from G. Burrows had appeared in the Burton Chronicle on 26 January 1893:

"The main thing which prevents a settlement is the payment of the boys. They say if they pay them they must reduce the price for getting coal two pence per ton. I think, if we say we will take a penny per ton less it will be about fair."

When the colliers eventually returned after giving up the strike, it was to find pinned up a list of those, including Joseph, who would not be accepted back. He took a job down the hill at Swadlincote, working for Thomas Wragg, makers of sanitary pipes. Pay was by the day and Joseph's weekly earnings in 1902 were £1 6s 6d, rising in August to £1

The daybook of William Payne, father of Joseph, relates to two regular clients of the public house. They were accustomed to paying off so much per week and one wonders how much was left of a workingman's wage for his wife and children.

M.Hull, m.s

10s when he took on different and heavier work with large-dimension pipes which, in a later age, would have been lift-assisted.

JOSEPH PAYNE: WAGE BOOK (1)

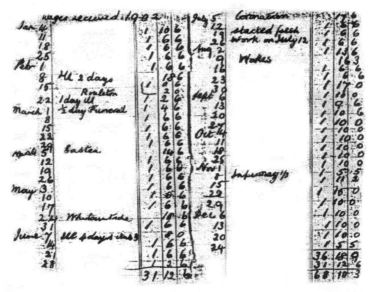

All periods of 'idleness' in 1902 had led to loss of pay, which applied equally to wakes (the annual holiday), illness, a hospital visit, funerals or the celebration of the new king's Coronation. Fresh work had brought a reward of 3s 6d per week.

A Liberal in politics like his father, Joseph had an interest extending to foreign as well as domestic issues. Attending a Conservative meeting in 1903, he noted a question he had asked about the import of pipes made in Belgium that was relevant to his own work for Wraggs. It was a period when each big political party – Tory and Liberal – tried to outdo the other over the question of tariffs. The Liberals were generally in favour of Free Trade, which might not benefit the working man if imports were undercutting the product

Wraggs Pipe Works on Coppice Side, Swadlincote

Pipes on display at Wraggs Pipe Works, Joseph Payne's workplace

227

of his own labour, while the Conservatives were pressing for a measure of protection.

It is interesting that, professionally, Joseph had no ambitions for advancement in the clay or any other industry, but that he was nevertheless a committed trades unionist: in the draft for a speech he would give in the run-up to the 1904 Swadlincote Council elections, he asked if the local employers had given the men any increase of wages during the first years of the new century,

'...so they could participate in the good times that the masters have had. I ask the masters to think of their men as human beings with lives to live and souls to save and pay them a fair living wage and not as so many machines to make money out of. If you treat a man as a man he will act honestly, but if otherwise what can you expect? Now I should like to say a word to the great body of men employed in this trade in this district. There is an army of workmen without a leader, nor organisation whatever among them and when things go wrong a little they are trampled and kicked by everyone. Would it not be better to organise and when the masters try to trample on you to stand shoulder to shoulder like men for your rights? How long are you going to take this punishment lying down?'

J. Payne m.s.

The election address that followed showed attention to practical local issues, as the result of which it might be said that a reading room followed within a decade, but another objective – a public park – took rather longer.

LOCAL GOVERNMENT:
Joseph Payne's Election Address (extract)
Swadlincote District Urban District Council Election 1904.
Church Gresley Ward.

Ladies and Gentleman

Having served you faithfully for nearly 4 years on the late School Board and being nominated for the District Council I now ask you for your support.

With respect to the common I should do my best to have it converted into a proper condition as a recreation ground for the benefit of the children of the District.

As we have heard so much about a Library I should do my utmost to obtain a reading room for the people of Gresley.

You will do me the greatest favour by attending the Poll on the 30th inst. And marking the voting paper opposite my name thus

                    Payne

                              Yours respectfully
                              Joseph Payne
                              78 Regent Street

                    Vote for Payne

The rhetoric of a Council election might be enough to get a Liberal candidate elected for the Gresley Ward on a working man's ticket, but national issues such as wage levels were likely to be affected more by events in Parliament and probably even more by the terms of trade and their impact on company balance sheets. There had been political developments, with the Labour Party winning seats in London and nearer home. The Borough of Derby seat had gone to the Liberals in 1900, and Labour had beaten the Conservatives into third place. South Derbyshire had traditionally been represented in Parliament by Burton's brewing family of Gretton, but the Liberal candidate H.H. Raphael had gradually cut into the Conservative lead and finally won in 1906 with a majority over John Gretton of 1,493. The union drive to improve conditions for

This 1912 postcard shows the striking miners hunting for "federation coal" that outcropped under the village of Newhall

workers in factory and mine had been ineffective and there was a push for Labour (which had won in Derby borough and in Belper in 1906) to field a candidate in South Derbyshire, even though that would split the anti-Tory vote.

At the workplace, Joseph and his mates were faced with the superior strength of their employers, which in 1912 led to defeat, despite a long and punishing six week strike, which brought no wage increase. The consequence was that Joseph took on a 6-day week, bringing him 5 shillings for working the extra day on Saturday.

Money was short, but good management could still make it go further. With his young daughter Lily, Joseph travelled by train and boat to the Isle of Man in 1894, touring the island, visiting a concert hall and bringing home the present of a shawl for his wife in Gresley.

Rail-Sea journey, Swadlincote-Douglas[1]
Isle of Man holiday 1894
(Joseph Payne with daughter Lily)

			£	s	d
July	31	Leaving box at station			2
		3 cups of tea			$4\frac{1}{2}$
		Dinners		2	4
		Fare Douglas and back		17	6
		Bread and sugar, Lily			6
		Soap 2, sweets 1			3
Aug	1	Bread 3, tomatoes 4			7
		Ferry fare			4
		Oysters			3
		Dinners		2	8
		Shave 2, chips $1\frac{1}{2}$			$3\frac{1}{2}$
		Bread 2, tomatoes 3			5
	2	Boots			4
		Bottle of beer			2
		Collection at dinner			3
		Bananas 3, ferry 1			4
	3	Fare to Ramsey		6	3
		Bread $2\frac{1}{2}$, grapes 6			$8\frac{1}{2}$
		Dinners		2	6
		Chips 3, tomatoes $2\frac{1}{2}$			$5\frac{1}{2}$
	4	Round island		8	9
		Bread $2\frac{1}{2}$, sausage $4\frac{1}{2}$			7
		Ferry 2, tomatoes 2			4
		Salts 5, hat 1/6		1	11
		Chips $2\frac{1}{2}$, shave 2			$4\frac{1}{2}$
	5	Stamp			$1\frac{1}{2}$
		Bottle of beer			2
		Dinners		2	4
		Bread 3, chips 2			5
		6 Lily's boots			2
		Groudle Glen		1	0
		Dinners		2	4
		Show 1/6, shawl 3/11		5	5
		Chips 2, tomatoes $1\frac{1}{2}$			$3\frac{1}{2}$
		Miss Kneele	1	13	0
			4	13	$10\frac{1}{2}$
		In hand	5	6	$1\frac{1}{2}$
			10	0	0

Right-hand totals column:

£	s	d
4	13	$10\frac{1}{2}$
5	6	$1\frac{1}{2}$
10	0	0

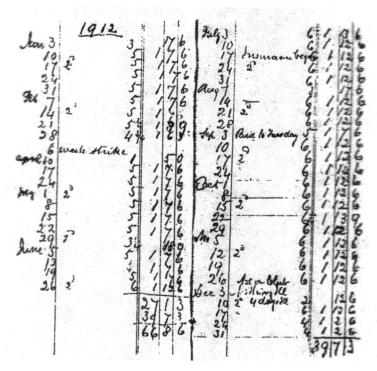

Joseph, in 1912, was being paid 5 shillings per day for his labour at Herbert Wragg's pipeworks. The strike that lasted with the ensuing lockout for the whole of March and the first few days of April led to a serious loss of income and, from the end of June, Joseph felt compelled to work Saturdays. In early December, he missed 10 days through illness. His daughter was to say, in later years, that her memory was of only strikes and wars. The biggest labour conflict, the General Strike, was in 1926 when Joseph had retired but her husband was 'out'.

About this time, Joseph had been with Lily's elder sister Maria to a Conservative meeting where the speaker had extolled the virtues of 'cheap money' quoting a figure of $3^{1}/_{2}$

per cent loans to be made available for mortgages. Maria's memoirs[2] relate that, at question time, Joseph said that 'he would like some of that'. His employer, who was chairman of the meeting, told Joseph to go along to the company office in the morning, where it was agreed that a loan would be made for 30 years – not at $3^{1}/2$ per cent but at 5 per cent and from this agreement, Joseph set about buying a piece of land in Regent Street, letting out five

Church Gresley's Police Constable, William Payne, son of Joseph, he lived in Pool Village, pictured here in 1905
© J. Payne

of the six houses erected there to his extended family.

CHURCH GRESLEY – HOUSING DEVELOPMENT C.1900[3]

Particulars of property as described on Form 4 sent in on Sept 24th 1910, No. 67 Regent Street. House with garden washhouse coalhouse closet and pigsty 255$^{1}/2$ yards.

	£	s	d
Yearly Rent	14	6	0
Land bought April 22nd 1897	33	0	0
Cost of Buildings	185	0	0
Street Markings	2	2	0

Land bought at a cost of 2s 6d per yard,
from Robert Heap.

The pigsty was a multiple-purpose facility, in which Joseph (brought up on a smallholding) reared pigs and his tenants (as here) kept chickens.

1 Joseph Payne papers.
2 M. Hull, op. cit., p. 5.
3 Joseph Payne papers.

CHAPTER 15

COMPETITION AND CONFLICT

AFTER THE GREAT WAR

The temper of society and of the domestic scene after 1918 was still, to the militant mind, disconcertingly normal. Despite the motor omnibuses crowding city streets Britain remained largely a horse-drawn economy. In Gresley's Regent Street, the only motor car, even in the late 1920s, belonged to the colliery manager and street lighting was by gas, its soft illumination kinder to the long terraces than electricity, which would have thrown them into harsher relief. The lamplighter did his rounds, morning and evening, preceded early in the day by the knocker-up ("five o'clock, Edwin!") calling on the sleeping worker who needed to get himself the two miles to Rawdon Colliery in time for its morning shift. Streets uncluttered by cars were a most convenient playground for children's games.

With few domestic appliances available at prices that they could afford, mothers had exacting routines of washing and cleaning, beginning with washing and drying on Monday, and ironing on Tuesday. The environment

Maria Payne (aged 22) and her brother Harry at their home in Church Gresley. Maria had just finished a year with a Worcestershire family as a schoolroom maid. Harry was to be a munitions worker in World War I

© J. Payne

suffered greatly from the smoke of a hundred chimneys serving clay-based industry, from which the worst hazard was the sulphur dioxide content of fumes from brick and pipe-makers. Water closets were not a standard fitment at the time for workers' houses and 'entries' inseparable from terraced housing of the period were designed to permit access by 'night-soil' operators – perhaps to the end of a garden.

In the 1920s, when work was plentiful, but offset by long hours and low wages, it was important to find inexpensive entertainment. Radio for most of the population became available only towards the end of the 1920s and even then it was a 'crystal-set' that was a part of the resources of the fortunate few, until it was superseded by the valve radio. These "wirelesses" were activated by lead batteries that had to be re-charged at the nearest power station in Swadlincote.

A Gresley pigeon fancier, 1905. The keeping of homing pigeons was well suited to the collier on shift work. It was usual for birds to be despatched in a wicker basket by rail with instructions as to station and time for their release

© M. Hull

The new century was marked by political events with social consequences. The Liberal H.H. Raphael's success in the 1906 parliamentary vote for the South Derbyshire constituency was part of a national trend. The division among the Tories over Free Trade versus Protection had been raised as an issue in Swadlincote at meetings of their local

Rawdon Colliery in the early 20th century before reconstruction

party. But more important, to many people, was the family budget of the manual and craft worker – this, at a time when women were without the vote. The Liberal leader Asquith had become Prime Minister in the 1908 Election, and in 1909 his Government introduced Old Age Pensions (7s 6d a week for a married couple, 5s for single people), making commitments to the retired that until then had been only debating points. For low-paid workers, the pension measure was a counter-blow against malign effects still lingering from early Victorian Poor Law legislation. But for men like Richard Edwin Hull, hoping in 1908 to marry, wages (£1 10s per week) were niggardly.

In 1911, Chancellor of the Exchequer David Lloyd George introduced National Insurance provisions under which employer and employee would contribute towards sickness and unemployment benefits. Such social legislation left untouched the great disparity in income between the upper and lower ranks of society and a reforming Labour Party, whilst increasing its representation at every General

Home made entertainment, Swadlincote's first Parade on 20th July 1912

Election, was still in a minority. Organised labour, through the trade unions, was pushing for wage improvements across whole industries, and when talking did not succeed, a national rail strike was called in 1911, followed the next year by a major coal strike. 1912 was an important year for Joseph Payne in his job with a Swadlincote pipe manufacturer. After involvement in a six-week strike that failed, Joseph extended his hours of all-day working on Saturdays with long-term consequences for his health, but in the third week of June 1912, he started contributions to the National Insurance scheme that would provide some cover for himself in sickness or unavoidable unemployment.

THE GREAT WAR

Britain declared war on Germany on August 4 1914, with the county cricket programme in full swing and Surrey soon to be declared champions. Greater events abroad were to transform the lives of all in the combatant nations. Volunteers flocked to the colours and shops were besieged with customers buying up essential foods: butter, margarine and sugar. Even so, the baker, without his usual 'fancies' still called with his basket the length of Regent Street and the milkman came every day with his open pail and measures going down to a gill. To replace men who had gone to France, the cry went out for munitions workers and Joseph Payne's son Harry, an engineer, went to work for BSA, making Mills bombs in the Black Country.

Housewives, managing already on small budgets, with no prospect of saving, were faced with food shortages, price rises and empty shelves in the shops that normally stocked basic foods. The cost of bread, by 1915, had risen to $8^1/2$d for a quarter loaf. In that year Richard Hull (Co-op membership number 5609) went to the Food Office in Swadlincote to collect a ration card, which he then took to the Church Street Co-op store for the family allocation of meat, butter and sugar. A registered retailer could not be changed without

William Harrison of the Royal
Marine Artillery in Egypt's Western
Front in 1918

William Harrison of Regent Street,
Church Gresley, photographed on
leave in the UK

© Courtesy his daughter Mrs M. McFetteridge

application to the issuing office.

In 1916 land was requisitioned to make available more allotments for local gardeners. In the same year, Prime Minister Asquith, moved by the great losses that had been suffered in France introduced conscription. In 1916 also, the Hull family's first-born, Richard Albert, was taken the short walk to start at the same York Road School where both of his parents had been taught. Albert, named after Queen Victoria's Consort, was given a present by his father on 24 May (Empire Day) 1916. It was a certificate from the Overseas Club, thanking the holder for sending 'some comfort to the brave Sailors and Soldiers of the British Empire' (shown in red on a map of the world, and very impressive). The local regiment was the Sherwood Foresters, but Robinsons employee William Harrison of Church Gresley, who had joined the Royal Marines, was in the Flanders trenches in the summer and autumn of 1917 during the terrible battles of Passchendaele. He also saw service at Mersa Matruh, in Egypt's Western Desert.

On the Home Front, by the start of 1918, many important items – margarine, eggs and tea – were in very short supply, but Joseph Payne had cause to feel content at the sight of the sides of bacon that hung curing from the ceiling of his kitchen/living room. Somehow using a system of barter he managed to find sufficient grain to feed his pigs. On the labour front, industrial relations had been frozen 'for the duration' after the Royal Proclamation of 1915, that made strikes illegal. Now workers in uniform were to return in militant mood from the trenches, having been assured by their Government that they would come back to a country 'fit for heroes to live in'.

THE GENERAL STRIKE, 1926

There had been many strikes in mines, at ports and on railways before and after the Great War. Although the first Labour Government in 1924 had been defeated over a case of alleged incitement to mutiny, after which Liberal support had been lost, there was increased militancy in the workplace. During the General Strike of 1926 there was a very large attendance on Gresley Common for the rally addressed by a national miners' figure A.J. Cook, and local union spokesmen. A threat to reduce their pay had concentrated the miners' resolve, but national action depended on the response of other workers and of their unions' governing body, the Trades Union Congress. The general action collapsed when middle-of-the-road trades union leaders, led by J.H. Thomas, sought a compromise with the Government. It was a move seen by many workers – not only miners – as needless retreat. Supporting unions returned to work whilst miners, in South Derbyshire and elsewhere, continued an

William Knight Smith, South Derbyshire's Miners' Agent (left) and Herbert Buck of Castle Gresley, assistant agent and checkweighman (right).
Both men were arrested for offences under Emergency Regulations during the 1926 strike (see p.248).
© Magic Attic Archive & Burton Mail Newspapers

isolated action for nearly six months.

The colliers were eventually forced back to work, their strike funds having been exhausted, the conditions for return being acceptance of lower wages and longer hours. During the dispute a solitary Regent Street miner had worked, returning home each afternoon, with police escort. There would be a daily accompanying crowd of opponents and spectators who included striking miners, their families and some of the children already home from school. One violent incident resulted in a near neighbour of the odd man out being sent to gaol.

The Conservative Government of the day, unsurprisingly, had strong views on the possibility of miners and their families 'benefiting' by extra relief during the period of the

There were scenes like these in Swadlincote throughout the day on
24 August 1926, when the South Derbyshire's miners' agent (see p.242) and
assistant agent were prosecuted and fined for alleged offences during the
General Strike. A section of the crowd in Belmont Street and High Street

The Crowd in West Street stretched many yards down the road, and
mounted police had to make a passage for traffic

strike. Neville Chamberlain, Minister of Health in 1926, secured the passage in the same year, of the Board of Guardians (Default) Act allowing him to take over direct control of the administration of poor relief in any unions where Guardians, it might have been judged, had 'defaulted' on their duties by being too liberal with aid for strikers' families.[1]

Pit Lane 1926

Oswald Hull describes the scene: "Pit Lane was normally a place of great activity – noisy, odorous (in the engine house one could not get away from the heavy, cloying, thick scent of lubricating oil) – all was very different on one morning in 1926. Beyond the pit bank leading far away from the colliery that fed it, many people were busy. Instead of the customary scene of wagons driven and pushed by light engines from the rattling screens, there was intense activity by coal pickers, re-sorting the material that the wagons had brought from the vicinity of the pithead. To the inferior coal and stone that the lads who worked the screens had discarded had been added still-hot ash, small timbers and other combustible material. Good or bad, the coal would ignite and wind would fan dull flames that burned day and night, in fine weather or foul, summer and winter. The bank's fires had a life of their own, nourished by interior heat. The monstrous perennial pile produced smoke habitually to drift over the lines of houses below, but now it was a resource on which the pickers drew.

Men, women and children clambered about the base and lower slopes, each equipped with a fork or probe with which to look for buried treasure. There would be some black, shiny, first-class pieces and much low-grade, but still acceptable material. Bagged and transported home, it would be given to friends or neighbours, family or workmates. A proportion was sold, bringing in important income. Employed as vehicles were handcarts, wheelbarrows, 'dandies' (home-made carts), pram bodies that could carry a surprisingly large load and bicycles across which filled sacks could be slung.

This was the 1920s and the immediate environment of the lane was uncommonly rural. Beneath the track's high hedgerows flourished a good variety of flowers: celandines, violets, red campion and an occasional deadly nightshade.

Originally a quiet country track leading to Mount Pleasant, Pit Lane had been widened since the sinking of Church Gresley Colliery, nearly a century before, to take horse-drawn coal-carts: it was rutted in a way that could happen only with the passage of heavy wheeled vehicles.

On the other side of the lane away from the pit bank was a second scene of great activity, not wholly different from the pickers' individualist efforts. In what had been green meadows, highly organised gangs, working to the discipline of the professional miner, brought to the surface coal that often lay but a short distance underneath. These were Federation men, working 'exposed' seams of coal that could elsewhere outcrop in miners' own gardens. In the fields, groups worked from trenches or squared-off pits reinforced against collapse of the encumbering yellow clay with old railway sleepers. There were many such discarded timbers by the Burton-Ashby railway line that ran in a tunnel beneath the lane. Where the men had gone down to a sufficient depth, there were headstocks and pulleys. Miners would pay the farmer a small rent and a share of the coal they dug; a much bigger traffic was taken away by lorry in a commercial operation from the larger enterprise on the Common, nearly a mile away. There, lorries queued up to take the Federation coal to power stations and business premises in Burton and further afield, where there was a desperate need for fuel."[2]

COAL AND THE COMMUNITY

Any extractive industry such as that covered in this book must decline and eventually come to an end – the speed of events affected by local conditions. The South Derbyshire-Leicestershire coalfield is a geological mix of exposed and

245

Coal Industry in South Derbyshire and Leicestershire[4]
Production and Employment 1913/1924-1937

Employment	Number of persons employed in coalmining														
	1913	1924	1925	1926	1927	1928	1929	1930	1931	1932	1933	1934	1935	1936	1937
Derbyshire, South	4,843	5,706	5,263	5,310	4,942	4,404	3,921	3,734	3,761	3,684	3,521	3,372	3,203	3,265	3,189
Leicestershire	10,327	12,556	11,843	11,938	11,536	11,343	11,305	11,079	10,935	10,812	10,312	9,773	9,272	9,205	9,052
notes				dispute											

Production	thousand tons														
	1913	1924	1925	1926	1927	1928	1929	1930	1931	1932	1933	1934	1935	1936	1937
Derbyshire, South	1,244	1,244 1,	112	679	1,048	896	926	878	816	730	690	712	748	806	842
Leicestershire	3,175	3,153	2,897	1,994	3,032	2,904	2,873	2,748	2,613	2,399	2,241	2,347	2,496	2,692	2,866
notes				dispute											

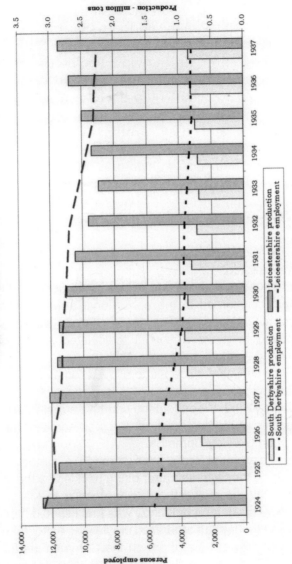

Coal Industry in South Derbyshire and Leicestershire

Production and Employment 1924-1937

Employment for 1926 represents numbers employed around 13th March. Most coal mines were idle much of the year due to a dispute which was initially supported by a General strike.

247

concealed measures, the last colliery in South Derbyshire having been sunk at Coton Park in 1912, although further to the west lie large reserves at increasing depth.

As production fell in the northern (Swadlincote-Newhall) area, it was compensated by a greater output on the Leicestershire border. In individual collieries, performance could depend on conditions underground peculiar to that pit, aggravated by what could have been profligate earlier exploitation. Some seams had been approached by operators seeking quick and easy profits. The graphs of coal production show output keeping up after World War I, but only with the help of a substantial increase in manpower that produced a reduction in output per man shift[3].

NEWSPAPER COVERAGE OF THE GENERAL STRIKE

AUGUST 12, 1926 [5]
Miners Arrested
Disturbances over the last few days in the South Derbyshire coalfield culminated in the sensational arrest of two well-known miners' leaders. They were charged with making or attempting to make a speech calculated to impede the supply and distribution of coal.

Only sufficient evidence to allow a remand until August 24 was given. Bail was allowed in substantial sureties.

Police-Supt. Wood told the court he arrested one of the defendants at his home, where the man admitted making a speech on Gresley Common.

His statement read: "Yes, I made a statement at a meeting on the Common after being heckled by the crowd. I was told by the crowd that it was coming to Marquis and Rawdon. The statement I made was that I should meet them because I thought an organized crowd was better than a dis-organized crowd. I met them on the Common the following day, and appealed to them not to go and not to do any damage. That was done in the presence of two constables".

A miners' agent was also charged with issuing a document calculated to delay the distribution of coal. He was remanded on bail until August 24.

Earlier in the week outcrop workers on Gresley Common had been evacuating their pits. On Monday morning a meeting was held round the workings and it was pointed out that a number of men had already "signed on" at regular pits because other were getting outcrop coal, and that if the mining of "Federation" coal was abandoned they would discontinue working at the pits.

As a result of this appeal a number of the outcrop workers removed their tackle and filled the shafts. The heavy, rain which fell during the week was another powerful inducement to adopt that course, for the water percolated through the soil and brought down the roots and made the headings unworkable. The result was that by the end of the week there were few outcrop pits in operation on the common.

Many lorries, from Burton, Derby and Leicester and other places made futile journeys to the Common for coal.

A later report stated the situation remained calm in South Derbyshire over the week-end, only the presence of big police patrols denoting that anything untoward had ever taken place.

On Saturday evening a large crowd attended a meeting on Gresley Common where a labour agent presided

CHURCH GRESLEY – OVERSEAL MAP

The O.S. map (original scale 6 inches to 1 mile) published in 1925, one year before the General Strike and two years before the last tramcar ran on the Burton to Ashby Light Railway, shows the tram route that led to a terminus at Gresley Station. A mineral line connected the Woodville branch of the Midland Railway to Church Gresley Colliery.

A feature of this area is the juxtaposition of industry and

farmland, with a major colliery on one side of Mount Pleasant Road ('Pit Lane') and Gresley Park Farm on the other. To the east of the railway tunnel and Swainspark is the terminus of the Ashby Canal. Benjamin Robinson, sanitary

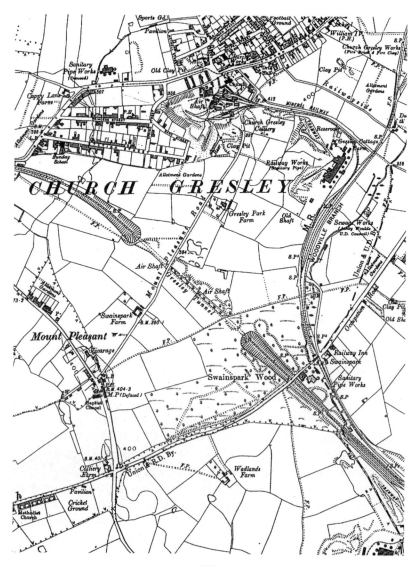

ware manufacturers, operated from the Church Works to the north of Gresley Colliery and parish church.

MOIRA COLLIERY Co., LIMITED,
BURTON-ON-TRENT.

No. 10250 CHURCH GRESLEY COLLIERY. May 9 1931

M .... Maur

TAKE NOTICE that you are to receive herewith
tons 10 cwt. qrs. of Butcha COAL.

	Tons.	Cwt.	Qrs.	Rate.	£	s.	d.
Weight of Coal and Vehicle	2	6	2				
Tare Weight of Vehicle	1	8	2	22/8	2	0	
Net Weight of Coal delivered to purchaser	10						
Weighed by					—	11	4
Carrier:	W. Maur			13	4		

When Coal is delivered by means of a vehicle the Seller must deliver or send by post or otherwise to the Purchaser or his servant, before any part of the Coal is unloaded, a Ticket or Note in this form.
Any Seller of Coal who delivers a less quantity than is stated on this Ticket or Note is liable to a fine.
Any Person attending on a Vehicle used for delivery of Coal who having received a Ticket or Note for delivery to the Purchaser, refuses or neglects to deliver it to the Purchaser or his servant, is liable to a fine.—52 and 53 Vic., c. 21, Weights and Measures Act, 1889.

Coal (pithead price £1 2s 8d per ton) was delivered by cart to the householder's address, the ticket shown here having been for half a ton (delivery charge two shillings).

At a period of time when there very few private cars the ton or half-ton of coal would be tipped in the street, to await the husband's return from his day's work. He would then wheel it by barrow to the coalhouse or coal shed at the rear of his dwelling.

AT THE COAL FACE

"...it was very hard work, when you worked your way through haulage work and got onto the coal face. You had a pick, a shovel and a hammer and you had to fill seven yards of Woodfield coal as they called it which could have been five foot high, four feet depth of cut and seven yards long. You used have to get the fireman to fire shots in it and you had to fill it out on the conveyor belt which took it to the pit bottom and then up the shaft in boxes. We never carried a lot of fat on us then. We were all lean."[6]

1 Reid, Andy, The union workhouse: a study guide for teachers and local historians, Phillimore: Chichester, 1994, p. 5.
2 O. Hull, m.s.
3 Statistical Abstract for the UK, 1939, HMSO.
4 Ibid.
5 Burton Mail
6 Out of the Dark: Swadlincote Stories, South Derbyshire Literature Development, 1998.
   The miner/writer worked first for Cadley Hill and then for Donisthorpe colliery.

CHAPTER 16

SOCIAL CHANGE AND A NEW WAR

Labour's national victory in 1929 was short-lived – a global infection of panic selling resulting in the failure of financial and trading institutions. Ramsay MacDonald and a few associates who had also been prominent in negotiations to end the General Strike, now moved to form a coalition – a 'National' Government – with members of other parties and in 1931 the official Labour Party was badly defeated when the General Election stood the 1929 result on its head. In 1931 also, the South Derbyshire industrialist Herbert Wragg again won Belper and in Ilkeston official Labour lost by two votes to National Labour. The Clay Cross by-election of 1933 saw the polarising and radicalisation of opinion with over 3,000 voting for a Communist. The life of the industrial communities continued with genuine hardship on many

The early 20th century brought important developments in adult education including the Swadlincote Mens Sunday Morning adult school shown here

streets and heavy reliance on the social provisions first introduced by Liberals. Their national Old-Age Pension had been set at 5s per week for those over 70 years of age with an annual income of less than £31 10s per year. The age for receipt of the pension was brought forward to 65 in 1925. National Insurance had been introduced, in 1911, by Lloyd George and a Labour Exchange set up in Swadlincote. All this provided a minimum measure of social security sufficient to stave off an explosion by those who, it might be thought, had been offered little charity in the past that was without stigma.

The events of 1926 did of course produce a big drop in output and great depletion of coal stocks. With the Depression years that commenced in 1929 there was a prolonged decline in production. The collapse of markets and of orders led to disturbing levels of unemployment, much of it in the form of short-time working. After 1936 a recovery in business and employment followed the placing of new orders in the domestic market, particularly in defence and related industries. With the rapid introduction of measures for mechanisation output per man shift improved, but at the same time conditions underground for miners working new faces could be very difficult. For instance at Church Gresley colliery in 1937-8 a shift could involve working a seam with pitch of 1 in 1.5. Movement 'along' the face involved not a walk but a slide, protected by leather reinforcement whilst manoeuvring between mini pit-props.

The means of getting such Derbyshire coal to market in the United Kingdom had improved during the life of Gresley Colliery. What had begun with a journey by tramway to Cut End, developed into a busy rail delivery mainly in a southerly or south-easterly direction via Leicester or Moira-Nuneaton. There was a ready market in London and the Home Counties for household fuel, but there was also growing demand from power stations needing small coal.

The biggest problem daily faced by the house-proud miner's wife was to cope with her man's need to wash away the accumulation of dust and grime inseparable from his job. A collier was always conspicuous at the end of a shift for his blackened face. The most welcome antidote before the end of the 1930s was the provision, largely with union money, of pit-head baths. The Potters' union was less fortunate in its pursuit of the issue of holidays with pay. The union supported the strike once the Potters' claim had been refused by sanitary pottery employers in Swadlincote-Church Gresley and Woodville in 1937, but the masters did not give way and the men returned to work without having won their holiday claim.

The author and his mother in 1934, at their home, formerly his grand-father's house in Church Gresley. © K.A. Hull

There was some change in the quality of life with the building of 'council' housing complete with W.C.s and lit eventually by electricity. Older houses had to wait until a landlord could negotiate improvements that were not too expensive for a tenant to afford. The consolidation of the economy and recovery in exports brought a slow addition to wage levels for Potters. It had been customary since the start of the century for the maker with his wheel to have a piece-work contract, purchasing the clay that he would fashion. Through the Thirties he had to pay for the floor to be swept, if he was to avoid choking clay dust at the close of work. The cost of gas used was extracted from his wages.

ENTERTAINMENT

There had been fairs and travelling entertainers far back into history. On the South Derbyshire coalfield after World War I, a growing population looking for escape provided a substantial market for the Holland family to set up their show each wakes week on Gresley Common, with stalls and swings, fortune-tellers and roundabouts, boxing booth and Big Top with circus artists. Essential to the feel of the special occasion was a splendid steam organ.

The demand for all-weather entertainment brought dramatic developments. The technology of filmmaking that had come from Europe at the very end of the 19th century sufficed to move the unique talent of Charles Chaplin from the music hall, to film. There was a great impetus for local enterprise to try its hand and at Swadlincote in 1913, Edwin Lawrence and Tommy Haines made their first film, *Parade* for the small Albion Film Company. After 1918, there was at least one performance per week at the town's Rink cinema, charging only a penny admission to see silent moving pictures, (or 'movies'). Their themes were romance, crime, drama or one of the early Chaplin classics. A silent film would be accompanied before each frame by a decorated title-card of dialogue – the young artist Alfred Hitchcock's introduction to cinema.

In 1928, the first part-talkie film, *The Jazz Singer*, with Al Jolson, that had opened the previous year in New York was shown in Swadlincote. *Ben Hur* was an early spectacular at the town's Empire cinema. A third Swadlincote cinema, the Majestic, complete with its own organ; was well patronised. In the words of a chronicler of these local cultural events:

> "For many the cinema was the only form of relief from work and sleep … there were few places to go except the cinema and of course many of the miners would be on permanent nights, so if they wanted to see a film the only time they could go would be in the morning. That's how miner's matinees came into being."

Out of the Dark, South Derbyshire Writers' Group, 1998.

The early part of the 20th century had brought important local developments in adult education, with the foundation of local branches of the Workers Educational Association, and the opening (funded by the William Carnegie legacy) of Swadlincote Public Library. The 1920s saw the inauguration at Swadlincote of the Gilchrist Lectures, held in the Town Hall. John Borthwick Gilchrist had been outstandingly versatile – a leading surgeon, businessman and Oriental linguist. The lecture courses in his name were promoted in Swadlincote by a mixture of industrialists, professional men and trades unionists: the local committee's chairman was Alderman Walter Jones. The Autumn 1929 lecture audience heard about "How the Cathedrals were Built" from the Dean of Norwich (aided by lantern slides) and "Bismarck," from Prof. A.J. Grant. In the 1920s, a more far-reaching aid to communication was the national daily newspaper – price 1d, printed in large provincial cities and in London. A local library such as Swadlincote's would be equipped with a reading room, where the popular newspapers were on display along with more serious journals, such as the *Manchester Guardian*, the *Birmingham Post* and *Sheffield Telegraph*. An uncomfortable thought: it was likely that, in the same room, many of the readers would be men for whom, on that particular day, there was no work.

After the Munich crisis of 1938, when Hitler met Prime Minister Chamberlain, serious preparations began to meet the prospect of a new war. Swadlincote, like other local authorities, drew up plans for defence against air attack. The question was, what form the threat to civilian population would assume. Recalling events in the Great War, in 1930 the airship R.100 had flown over South Derbyshire, only for its sister-ship the R.101 to be consumed by fire later the same year. Though the German Zeppelin Hindenburg was also destroyed in 1939, it was felt that any threat would come from a resurgent German airforce.

WORLD WAR II

1939 was different from 1914, if only because a Great War had gone before. The machinery of mobilisation had, as it were, just to be oiled for a nation to be armed more quickly than before. But things had moved on: whereas the first World War had started with a volunteer army going to the Front, immediate measures were taken in 1939 to call up classes of men who had been passed fit. Several young men from Ashby Grammar School, including the author, who had begun degree courses at Oxford, found themselves in the same training camp of the Oxford and Bucks. Light Infantry at Cowley Barracks.

September 29 1939 was National Registration Day, when forms were filled in, enabling everyone to be issued with a national identity card and then with a ration book – the first card giving access to the other. It was not long before leaflets were distributed in South Derbyshire or printed in local newspapers telling the population what to do in a variety of emergency situations. Everywhere one went, on the first morning of war, there were people who had followed the official instruction to sling a gas mask over the shoulder before going out. On the way from Gresley Parish Church to Swadlincote one passed the memorial to the Great War, with men in uniform going to fight the next one.

The calm before the storm: the author and his mother in the Old Quad of Hertford College, Oxford, 1939
© K.A. Hull

In World War I, poison gas had been introduced by both sides and there was apprehension, indicated by the initial issue of gas masks to the public, that poison gas might be dropped over Britain: hence the message in 1940 in Public Information Leaflet no. 6: 'If you have any suspicion that food or water has been affected by poison gas notify an Air Raid Warden or the police immediately.'

Gas attack did not happen, but when the 'phoney war' in Western Europe ended in 1940 and the expected air raids over Britain cities commenced in the summer of that year, the public soon became accustomed to the nightly procession over the South Derbyshire coalfield of enemy aircraft – their approach signalled by the characteristic throb of the engine of a Junkers 88 bomber. Targets were the industrial centres of Derby, Manchester and Merseyside, the route involuntarily lit by the glow of active kilns that could not be concealed.

Derby, the significant Luftwaffe target in the region covered by this book, had a long-established engineering base and the LMS rail workshops helped produce the chassis for rail-mounted howitzers, using drawings left over from World War I. Qualcast, manufacturer of lawn-mowing equipment, was converted to the production of hand grenades and a large proportion of the additional workforce taken on were women – an example of roles changed by a war situation. In another department of the LMS complex, women worked on the tail and fuselage sections of new aircraft, whilst at Spondon, in the British Celanese factory, men and women worked together on the manufacture of parachutes. At Alvaston, women members of the WAAF sewed barrage balloons.[1]

A new extension of trolleybus services southwards out of Derby took workers to the greatly extended Rolls Royce aero-engine factory on Sinfin Moor. The demands for increased production were unrelenting. On 6 November, 1943, women over 50 registered in Derby for war work and civilians travelled long distances to the factories by bus or train whether to Derby or to the army depot at Branston outside Burton-on-Trent. Typical of the commuters was the girl from Swadlincote[2] who journeyed to the Burton works of B.T.R., a subsidiary of ICI, making radiators for aeroplanes. She worked 60 hours a week, on a routine of 14 days of nightwork, followed by a similar period of days; the pay was £3 per week. It was ICI who moved the Swadlincote worker and five other girls to a Holiday Fellowship hostel near Doncaster, from where they worked a three-shift system in a

URBAN DISTRICT OF SWADLINCOTE DISTRICT.

Air Raid Precautions.

This is to Certify that the Bearer

Miss Kathleen A. Hull.

is an Air Raid Warden for the

URBAN DISTRICT

OF

SWADLINCOTE DISTRICT.

E. K. Alce.
Clerk.

factory making cordite explosives for shells. With their ration books the workforce bought each week, 2 ounces of butter, margarine, about 3 ounces of bacon, 2 ounces of sweets and dried eggs. A Ministry of Food recipe for economy Christmas stuffing consisted of ¹/₂lb of sausage meat, to which were added prunes, onion, chopped apple or apple rings and 2 dried eggs, (reconstituted) with thyme and seasoning.[3] Families, and war workers alike were affected by events.

SOUTH DERBYSHIRE AT WAR – 1941[4]

Maria Hull writes

Friday Jan 3rd 41
A terribly cold day. N.E. wind went out shopping posted letter to E. was unable to get steak for Father also 4d liver, not any cheese at the Co-op stores this week. ¹/₂lb for 2 people only when they do have it that has prevailed this last few weeks. Kathleen came, we had chips & liver for dinner. K. brought 2lbs of oranges and lemons. She took photos. I dressed up for the occasion too. An alert again I have heard bombs exploding.

Sat 4th 1941
A very sharp frost but not so severe as yesterday. I made "potato apple cake" sent two to K. by Hetty: 2 eggs from Wm Smith 7¹/₂d. Sprouts 3d lb. Cooking apples 6¹/₂d lb controlled price. Also I made mincepies, all mince-meat now used up. An alert sounded at 1

261

a.m. I did not get up. All clear went at 2.30. a little later an alert sounded in another district. Not able to sleep I got up at 3 o'clock & took a pot of tea upstairs. We each had some, I hugged the tea-pot, it's a good warmer.

Thursday 9th

An air-raid warning sounded 7.30p.m. It was anticipated by the good conditions of the weather. It's a lovely moonlight night. The procession of planes on their raiding bent kept up till 1 o'clock when I went to bed. The all clear went at 1.45. T. Hancock has made a coal bunk for K. It is strong enough for the high seas.

Wednesday 15th

The ground white over with snow this morning & it is very cold. No beef at Dents. I got a pig's foot 2d & 2 lambs kidneys 2d each. Edgar Hall has been buried today. he was killed when on an F.S.[5] duty at Liverpool a fortnight ago. It is now 11.20p.m. an air raid warning sounded over 2hrs ago. the Naval Gun at Derby keeps banging, making one jump. A lot of planes have gone over. I made a seed cake & buns to-day. No enemy planes. during the day they are now making up for it. I feel sure they must be trying to get in at Derby by the banging of that Gun. I will now have a cup of tea. the all clear went at 1.20. I retired to bed woke up about 3 o'clock planes passing over the noise was terrible.

Tuesday 21st

A thaw set in during last night. I felt the difference in bed. it is not so cold. What a quantity of snow has come to be sure. a great number of people have cleared it away in front of their house. Ours was cleaned away before I got down-stairs this morning. The baker came after tea to-day. An alert was sounded at 3.15 this afternoon lasted $\frac{1}{2}$ hour. Father has heard that 5 passengers the guard of the train standing in the station at Derby, 2 porters, & a station police-man were killed, & 40 people injured last Wednesday when the bomb fell.

Tuesday April 4th
I've not felt well to-day depressed again. However I got done through & took a walk after tea, calling on Mrs. Arthur. Geoff very unexpectedly came home last night much to his mother's relief. Their ship struck a wreck and put it out of gear, so had to come back to Liverpool for repair. She will not feel so upset now that she has seen him before he goes abroad.

Thursday 10th April
I haven't done much beside rest & knit, Kathleen came after tea. Another raid warning before 10 o'clock. Coventry was badly bombed again. Billy Harrison attested at Derby joined the navy, Royal Marines.

Good Friday April 11th
We did not have the customary fish dinner but a small piece of veal stuffed which I kept over from the weekend, curly greens, baked potatoes & ground rice pudding with damsons. I got up at 1.15 in the night & stayed up for about 2 hours. K. had told me not to disturb her but I was really nervous & quite expected to be ready for going under the table. Such a lot of gunfire I could hear & planes going over again. K. gone back to Stanton.

PEACEFUL PROGRESS

A different Government was returned to power in 1945, with a new M.P. for South Derbyshire – represented by P.V. Emrys-Evans since 1931. In his election address, the sitting member had warned against the creation of 'monopolies, for they restrict enterprise and crush the small man'. His voice was not heeded by the voters.

A.J. Champion. Labour.	47,586
P.V. Emrys-Evans. Conservative.	24,636
N. Heathcote. Liberal	10,255
Labour majority	22,950

The Liberals were humbled, but that seemed less important than the landside move towards Labour, even in normally safe Conservative seats such as Burton, with its tradition of brewery-based M.P.s. Labour set out to nationalise much of the country's economy. Flags went up over local pits on New Year's Day 1947, as the property of the Moira Colliery Company and other coal owners was nationalised. A year later, in January 1948, more flags were flying, as the railways were taken into public ownership. From now on, trades unions would negotiate pay with national boards in charge of their industries. Electricity, including the coal-fired power generated in the Trent valley, was taken over.

Police Constable Vyse (right) pictured with a colleague in Ilkeston 1925. He went on to become Linton's policeman from 1932-1948 and retired there to run a local pub

© Courtesy of H.L. Sills

Perhaps the most penetrating part of the new order came on 5 July 1948, with the introduction of a National Health Service that was particularly good news for those on lower incomes. Consumer problems remained for some years after the war, with bread continuing on the ration until July 1948 and sugar until September 1953. Clothes rationing had ended in March 1949 – a relief to men who had hung on to the suit

The growth of motor transport can be clearly seen in this early 1950s scene in Swadlincote High Street

Even post World War II Church Gresley's Market Street could be completely free of motor traffic

War Memorial Gates, Swadlincote Park

that they had been given on demobilisation. In 1942 Sir
William Beveridge had produced the report which, after the
war, made a major difference towards building what came to
be known as a Welfare State, with its attendant structure of
social services affecting most of the population. Benefits and
allowances were distributed from new offices centrally
situated in towns and urban centres such as Swadlincote.
There would still be inequalities and huge differences in the
living standards of rich and poor but the case for a new level
of government intervention had been made.

The war with Hitler ended with animated discussion on
the nature of society and the future of education. There was
a widespread feeling that the primary school children who
had failed pre-war selection tests had included many with
unrecognised ability. The Labour Party Conference of 1942[6]
had called for the development of a new type of secondary
school that would cater for the whole range of talent. This
objective underlay the comprehensive idea that was to
become persuasive, not only among teachers.

Official thinking moved slowly and began only by changing titles, so that staff returning from the war found that senior elementary schools had been renamed secondary modern.[7] The first comprehensive schools in the district came in a burst of activity: the all-ability Granville School opened at Woodville in 1958 and the William Allitt County Secondary School at Newhall in 1959. Pingle High School followed at Swadlincote on 2 July 1966. Comprehensive education had arrived.

From Pingle's Sixth Form biology class, Alan Wolffe of Castle Gresley went up to Keble College, Oxford. After receiving a degree in bio-chemistry in 1982, he married Elizabeth Hall, from Woodville, who had been in the same class at Pingle before going on to gain her degree at Birmingham University. The couple moved to the United States but Dr. Alan Wolffe having gone on business to Rio de Janeiro in 2001, was tragically knocked down and killed whilst jogging.

THE REGION'S CHANGING FACE

After the Local Government Act of 1972, the local authority changed its name from Swadlincote Urban District Council to South Derbyshire District Council, to take in the former Urban District to which were added Repton Rural District and part of South East Derbyshire Rural District. The election of members to the new Council was held on 7 June 1973 and its first meeting took place at the Poplars, Rolleston Road, Burton-on-Trent, on 25 June 1973. New council offices, officially opened on 18 February 1977, were subsequently much extended.

The face of the coalfield was drastically changed by the end of deep mining. Cadley Hill, in 1988, was the last South Derbyshire colliery to close: it was only three years after miners had returned to work following the national coal strike of 1984-5. Whilst employment contracted in the south of the region, further north staff were being recruited for a

Looking down on Swadlincote from the new Ski Slope with Woodwards
factory chimney dominating the sky line 1999

Photo: Eric Matthews

very different industry. The Toyota Motor Corporation had
chosen a site outside Burnaston to build their European Car
Assembly Plant, where production started on 1 December
1992.

Most of the colliery banks are grassed over and some clay
holes have been filled or disguised. The contours of other
former diggings have been used to build a ski centre – a new
role for what had once been Common land.

1 Derby Daily Telegraph, 'World at war' for detail on the Derby region.
2 M. Bennett, m.s., author's papers.
3 Burton Observer, Dec. 21 1944.
4 M. Hull, m.s.
5 Fire-service.
6 Armytage, W.H.G., Four Hundred Years of English Education,
   Cambridge University Press, 1965, p. 316.
7 Dent, Harold Collett, The Educational System of England and Wales,
   University of London Press, 1961, p. 118.

BIBLIOGRAPHY

PRINTED SOURCES

BOOKS

Armytage, W.H.G., *Four Hundred Years of English Education*, Cambridge University Press, 1965.

Ashton, T.S., *The Industrial Revolution 1760-1830*, 1948.

Austerberry, Jennie, *Chad, Bishop and Saint*, English Life Publications: Derby, 1984.

Beaumont, P., *History of the Moira Collieries*, Bemrose & Sons: Derby & London, 1919.

Brayshaw, A. Neave, *The Personality of George Fox*, Allenson & Co: London, 1933.

Chambers, Jonathan David & Mingay, Gordon Edmund, *The Agricultural revolution, 1750-1880*, B.T. Batsford: London, 1966.

Cheney, C.R., *Episcopal visitation of monasteries in the thirteenth century*, Manchester University Press, 1983.

Cox, John Charles, *Notes on the Churches of Derbyshire*, 4 vols., Bemrose & Sons: London & Derby, 1875-9.

Cox, John Charles, *Three Centuries of Derbyshire Annals*, 2 vols., Bemrose & Sons: London & Derby, 1890.

Dent, Harold Collett, *The Educational System of England and Wales*, University of London Press, 1961.

Eden, Sir Frederick Morton, *The State of the Poor*, 3 vols., London, 1797.

Farey, John, *General view of the agriculture and minerals of Derbyshire*, 3 vols., London, 1811-17.

Floud, Roderick & McCloskey, Donald N., (eds.), *Economic History of Britain since 1700*, 2 vols., Cambridge University Press, 1994.

Fryer, Jonathan, (ed.), *George Fox and the children of the light*, Kyle Cathie, c.1991.

Glover, Stephen, *The History of the County of Derby*, 2 vols., H. Mozley & Son: Derby, 1829.

Green, H., *Child Labour in the Coal Mines of Nottinghamshire and Derbyshire in the 19th century: Extracts from the Reports of Commissioners*, 1842, Derbyshire Archaeological Society, 1936.

Gregg, Pauline, *A social and economic history of Britain 1760-1980*, Harrap, 1982.

Griffin, A.R., *The British Coalmining Industry: Retrospect and Prospect*, Moorland Publishing Co: Buxton, 1977.

Hadfield, Ellis Charles Raymond, *Canals of the East Midlands*, David & Charles: Newton Abbott, 1966.

Hadfield, Charles, *Canals of the West Midlands*, David & Charles: Newton Abbott, 1985.

Hammond, J.L. & Barbara, *The Town Labourer, 1760-1832*, Longmans, 1978.

Harrison, J.F.C., *Early Victorian Britain, 1832-51*, Fontana: London, 1979.

Hayek, F.A. (ed.), *Capitalism and the Historians*, Routledge & Kegan Paul: London, 1954.

Jones, W.L.P., *The trade in lunacy: a study of private madhouses in England in the eighteenth and nineteenth centuries*, Routledge & Kegan Paul: London, 1972.

Kitching, Colin (ed.), *Squire of Calke Abbey: Extracts from the journals of Sir George Crewe of Calke Abbey, South Derbyshire, 1815-1834*, Scarthin: Cromford, 1995.

Leleux, Robin, *A Regional History of the Railways of Great Britain, Vol. 9: The East Midlands*, David St. John Thomas: Newton Abbot, 1984.

Mackay, Thomas, *The History of the English Poor Law*, 3 vols., P.S. King & Son: London, 1904.

Madan, Falconer, *The Gresleys of Drakelow: An account of the family*, Oxford, 1899.

Oxley, G.W., *Poor Relief in England and Wales, 1601-1834*, David & Charles, 1974.

Pilkington, James, *A view of the present state of Derbyshire*, 2 vols., William Marriott: Derby, 1789.

Porter, Roy, *English Society in the Eighteenth Century*, Penguin, 1990.

Reid, Andy, *The union workhouse: a study guide for teachers and local historians*, Phillimore: Chichester, 1994.

Salter, Rev. H.E. (ed.), *Chapters of the Augustinian Canons*, London, 1922.

Spavold, Janet (ed.), *In the name of God, amen: Everyday life in South Derbyshire, 1535-1700*, South Derbyshire Local History Research Group: Ashby de la Zouch, 1992.

Spavold, Janet *At the sign of the Bulls Head: a history of Hartshorne and its enclosure*, South Derbyshire Local History Research Group: Woodville, 1985.

Stenton, F.M., *Anglo-Saxon England*, Oxford University Press: Oxford, c. 1971.

Sylvester-Bradley, P.C. & Ford, T.D. (eds.), *The Geology of the East Midlands*, Leicester University Press: Leicester, 1968.

Tuke, Daniel Hack, *Chapters in the history of the Insane in the British Isles*, Kegan Paul: London, 1882.

Vinogradoff, Paul, *English Society in the 11th Century*, Oxford University Press, 1908.

Webb, Sidney & Beatrice (eds.), *Minority Report of the Poor Law Commission*, 2 vols., Longmans, 1909.

Woodward, G.W.O., *The Dissolution of the Monasteries*, Blandford Press: London, 1966.

Worrall, E.S., *Returns of Papists, 1767*, Vol. 2, Catholic Record Society: London, 1989.

ARTICLES

Chandler, T.J., *Communications and a Coalfield: a study in the Leicestershire and South Derbyshire Coalfield Transactions*, Institute of British Geographers, 1957, pp. 163-172.

Crewe, Sir George, *A Word for the Poor*, Address to both Houses of Parliament 1803.

Dalton, R.J., *Agricultural Change in South Derbyshire 1800-1870*, East Midland Geographer Vol. 20, 1997.

Felkin, W., *History of machine-wrought hosiery*, Com. Journal no. xxxvii, 1867.

Holmes, W.D., *The Leicestershire and South Derbyshire Coalfield: The Coal Mining Industry*, East Midland Geographer Vol. 10, December 1958.

Holmes, W.D., *The Leicestershire and South Derbyshire Coalfield: The Clay Industry*, East Midland Geographer Vol. 12, December 1959.

Holmes, W.D., *The Leicestershire and South Derbyshire Coalfield: Light Industry*, East Midland Geographer Vol. 13, December 1960.

Hull, Oswald, *Gresley – The Family, lands and Priory*, Derbyshire Archaeological and Natural History Society, 1959.

Unpublished Thesis

Hillier, Kenneth, *The Welfare and Education of working-class children in Ashby-de-la-Zouch in the Nineteenth Century* (to 1980), Dissertation for the Degree of MA in English Local History, 1996.

Swadlincote Library

Bradford, J.T., *A lifetime in Linton – boyhood in a Derbyshire mining village in the 1920s*, published by Sylvia Bradford, 2001.

Greening, B., *A short history of 'The Streets' in Castle Gresley*, 1996.

Hull, Maria, *Growing up in Derbyshire in the Nineteenth Century*, published by Oswald Hull, 1986.

Out of the Dark: Swadlincote Stories, South Derbyshire Literature Development, 1998.

Into the Light: More Swadlincote Stories, South Derbyshire Writers' Group, 2000.

The British Library, Euston Rd, London

British Parliamentary Papers.

Select Committee Reports on Agricultural Distress; Enclosure; Farm Employment of Women and Children; Justice and Prisons; Irish University Press (also in Derbyshire Libraries).

Victoria History of the County of Derbyshire, 2 vols., London, 1905 (later known as Victoria County History [VCH], also in Derbyshire Libraries).

English Historical Documents series. Official papers include material on the Reformation and 18th-19th century measures for relief.

Letters and Papers, Foreign and Domestic, Henry VIII (also in Nottingham University Library).

Archival Material

Family Records Centre, Islington, London

1851 Census Returns for Union workhouses
Ashby de la Zouch – HO 107/2084
Burton upon Trent (Horninglow) – HO 107/2012
Shardlow – HO 107/2140

1851 Census Return for Walsall Borough
William Waring – HO 107/2023
Ann Waring (wife) – ditto

LOCAL ARCHIVAL SOURCES

Collier, R.E., *Notes on History of Shardlow, Collection of Jeff Clifton*, Shardlow History Group.

Hall, Maurice: papers from employment at National Coal Board's divisional headquarters at Coleorton Hall.

White, P.M. & Storer, J.W., *Around the Wooden Box*, 1984, History of Woodville industries.

CHARTERS

Jeayes, I.H., *Charters and Muniments of the Marquis of Anglesey*, William Salt Archive Society, Stafford (after 1939, Staffordshire Record Society).

Rydeware Charters; Phillipps Charters – originals held by John Rylands Library, Manchester (translations at Swadlincote Library).

Confirmation Charter Gresley Church & Priory, 1268, original held at Henry E. Huntington Library & Art Gallery, San Marino, CA, USA (typescript translation at Swadlincote Library).

NATIONAL ARCHIVES, KEW, SURREY

Poor Law Unions – records concerning the Unions and Workhouses of Ashby-de-la-Zouch, Burton-on-Trent and Shardlow – contained in boxes with MH12 or MO12 index numbers.

Extensive library of sources for the English Reformation and Poor Laws.

DERBYSHIRE RECORD OFFICE, MATLOCK

Series of Derbyshire Deeds – medieval period to present day.

Gresley Papers – medieval period to 19th century.

Parish Registers – c.1540 to present day.

Overseers of the Poor accounts (from 1790).

Churchwardens' accounts (from 1774).

Ms maps, 16th century to 20th century.

Official records of the county – 16th century to 20th century.

INDEX

277